# BUILDING WEALTH THROUGH REAL ESTATE:

A Guide to a Multi-Million Dollar Real Estate Investing Career

Written by

Dr. Ebony McArthur

**COPYRIGHT © 2023 BY AUTHOR**

All rights reserved.
No portion of this book may be reproduced in any form without written permission from the publisher or author, except as permitted by the copyright law.

**Printed by:**

The Werking Mom, LLC

Printed in the United States of America

**First Printing Edition, 2023**

ISBN 979-8-218-21840-9

# TABLE OF CONTENTS

INTRODUCTION..........................................................
BUILDING WEALTH THROUGH .................................1
REAL ESTATE .................................................................1
CHAPTER 2...................................................................... 6
WHAT THEY DON'T TELL YOU ABOUT INVESTING IN ........ 6
REAL ESTATE .................................................................6
CHAPTER 3......................................................................16
DEVELOPING YOUR ....................................................16
MILLIONAIRE CONFIDENCE ......................................16
MASTERING THE BRRRR STRATEGY .......................24
CHAPTER 5......................................................................41
HOW TO PAY FOR YOUR BRRRR ..............................41
BUILDING WEALTH THROUGH .................................49
REAL ESTATE ...............................................................49
CHAPTER 7......................................................................56
WHOLESALING THE ....................................................56
"QUICK CHECK" ...........................................................56
CHAPTER 8......................................................................64
FIX & FLIP THE "FAT CHECK" ....................................64
BUY & HOLD THE ........................................................76
"FOREVER CHECK" .....................................................76
CHAPTER 10....................................................................87
FINDING & EVALUATING PROPERTIES: THE DIAMOND IN THE ROUGH...................................................................87
CHAPTER 11....................................................................96
HOW TO USE .................................................................96
OTHER PEOPLES MONEY (OPM)................................96

# INTRODUCTION

Welcome to the real estate investing world. I hate to be the one to break it to you, but it's not going to be a smooth sailing ride. But what I do know is that once you've learned how to walk in real estate, you're going to be running towards a secure future and becoming a real estate investor. Your journey through real estate and becoming a real estate investor begins by taking it step by step, and that's why I'm here to guide you along the way. Real estate investing has several benefits. Investors can benefit from residual cash flow, outstanding return on investment percentages, tax advantages, and diversification. It is possible to use real estate as a tool to build and increase wealth. Are you considering investing in real estate? What you need to know about real estate investing and the benefits of building wealth through real estate is provided here.

Most millionaires I've met made more money off investing in real estate than any other type of investment. Real estate is less susceptible to short-term volatility due to the stock market and is sought out by many investors as a more long-term stable investment strategy. Whether you choose to purchase a home or rent an apartment or commercial building for profit, you obtain a real, functional asset that can be passed down from generation to generation.

Any moment is a great opportunity to invest in real estate, and the sooner the better. In truth, money is created by making purchases when everyone else is making sales and vice versa. While there is general talk of a recession looming, the real estate market is still strong, with rising prices and transactions.

A $1 million home might be yours for just $5,000 a month in loan payments, whereas a one-bedroom apartment can cost up to $6,000 a month to rent in desirable areas today. No matter the state of the economy, real estate will always be an excellent investment since there is an innate demand for housing. So, if you're up for the challenge, stay put, and let's begin.

# CHAPTER 1
# BUILDING WEALTH THROUGH REAL ESTATE

Are you tired of living from paycheck to paycheck and feeling like you can't reach your financial goals? Getting rich through real estate could be the answer you've been looking for. With the right plans, anyone can use real estate investments to build a path to financial freedom. Whether you've been investing for a long time or just getting started, these tips will help you take your real estate portfolio to the next level and reach your financial goals. So, let's get started and find out how to do well in real estate investing.

**Stay Disciplined With Your Finances**

One of the most important things you can do to build wealth in real estate is to be responsible with your money. Investing in real estate requires a lot of money upfront, especially for new investors, and it can be tempting to spend too much or take on too much debt. But you need to be very disciplined if you want to be able to handle market changes, unexpected costs, and other financial setbacks. When it comes to making money in real estate, discipline means watching how much you spend, thinking carefully about potential investments, and not taking on too much debt. This means doing your research on possible investments, thinking about each property's long-term potential, and avoiding high-risk investments that could cause you to lose a lot of money. Being disciplined with your money also keeps you from making decisions on the spur of the moment that could hurt your finances and make it harder for you to build wealth in the real estate market.

## Maximizing Leverage

Leverage is a proven strategy to build wealth in real estate because it lets you get the most out of your investments by borrowing money to buy more properties or properties with higher returns. Using other people's money and taking advantage of tax breaks and lower borrowing costs are all ways this strategy can help you make more money. For example, if an investor puts down $100,000 on a property worth $500,000 and the property's value goes up to $600,000, the investor gets back not only the $100,000 they put down but also $100,000 on the $500,000 increase in the property's value. But it's important to remember that using leverage can also increase risk if the investment doesn't do as expected. It's important to have a good understanding of the financial market and to carefully plan and manage your investments. Overall, using leverage to its fullest extent can be a powerful way to build wealth in real estate, but it needs careful planning, research, and risk management to work.

## Be Patient

Building wealth in real estate can be a long-term investment strategy, and patience is one of the most important things you can do to be successful. Getting a good return on an investment in real estate takes a long time and a lot of patience. By waiting, you give your investment time to grow and become more valuable, which can lead to a big rise in value over time. When you invest in real estate, being patient also helps you make decisions that are based on facts. Rushing into investments can cause you to make hasty decisions that can cost you a lot of money. With patience, you have time to look into and compare different properties so you can make smart choices that can lead to good returns.

**Focus On Cash-Flow**

Focusing on cash flow is a tried-and-true way to build wealth in real estate because it provides a steady source of income that can be re-invested in other properties, which grows the overall portfolio. When an investment property has a positive cash flow, it means that the rental income is more than the costs of owning it, such as the mortgage, property taxes, insurance, maintenance, and repairs. This steady flow of cash is a powerful tool for building wealth over time. It gives investors a safety net and lets them ride out short-term changes in the market. The extra cash flow can be used to pay off debt, buy more properties, or invest in other areas. By focusing on cash flow, you can get a steady stream of income from your properties, which you can use to buy more properties or pay off your mortgages faster. This helps you build wealth over time and gives you a reliable source of passive income that can help you become financially independent and free.

## Continuously Educate Yourself

This helps you keep up with the latest market trends, changes in the industry, and new investment opportunities. By keeping up with news and information, you can make better investment decisions and increase your chances of being successful. Education can also help you understand the different parts of real estate investing, such as property management, financing options, and market analysis, which can increase your chances of making money in this field. Regularly attending workshops, classes, and conferences can be a great way to stay up to date and keep learning about the real estate field. You can also keep up with changes in regulations, tax laws, and other things that can affect your real estate investments by continuing your education. If you know a lot about the latest industry trends and rules, you can make smart investment decisions that'll help you reach your financial goals and reduce your risks.

## Network & Build Relationships

Due to the numerous benefits it offers to real estate investors, developing relationships and a network is a tried-and-true method for increasing wealth in the industry. You may have access to special offers that are not open to the general public if you have strong ties with real estate professionals like brokers, agents, and lenders. In conclusion, developing your network and relationships can help you access better investment options, boost your knowledge and reputation, and make it easier for you to acquire funding, making it a crucial strategy for accumulating real estate wealth. Building relationships involves more than just growing your network; it also involves fostering and upholding those connections. You must be sincere, respectful, and reliable. Respect your contacts, help them out when you can, and be prepared to reciprocate. It takes time and work to develop solid relationships, but in the long term, it can result in additional chances, better offers, and a more satisfying real estate profession.

**Take Calculated Risks**

Because it entails evaluating a prospective investment opportunity and measuring the potential advantages against the potential hazards, taking calculated risks can be one of the tested ways to accumulate wealth in real estate. Investors can find high-reward investments with the potential for significant returns by taking controlled risks and by making strategic investments that are in line with their long-term investment objectives. Yet, it's crucial to keep in mind that taking risks necessitates being ready for any losses and having a strategy in place to handle these losses should they arise. Real estate investors might benefit from high returns and eventually reach their financial objectives by taking sensible risks.

## CHAPTER 2
# WHAT THEY DON'T TELL YOU ABOUT INVESTING IN REAL ESTATE

As you might imagine, real estate can be a long-term investment. So, the key is to make sure you understand what to expect and the risks involved in making such a large investment; it's important to gain as much information as possible. However, there are many things that investors don't necessarily realize about investing in real estate.

Investing in real estate can be a rewarding strategy to increase your income, stabilize your finances, and a means to wealth building. A typical American with an average income, however, might find the idea of purchasing an investment property completely out of their reach. Many people believe that wealthy people are the only ones who can afford to invest in real estate. However, that is not the case anymore. Even if you don't have much cash on hand, you can invest in real estate to amass a sizable fortune and develop a portfolio of assets that can be passed down to your children and grandchildren.

You don't even have to always utilize all of your own money to make money in real estate, even though having some of your own money is necessary. You can use other people's money to acquire real estate if you're resourceful enough. In fact, saving up a sizable down payment for years is not necessary.

Other people's money (OPM) is a term used in real estate to describe employing leverage to purchase real estate. You might not have the cash on hand or the credit to finance your property investments if you are just starting in real estate investing. However, here are a few of the ways you can invest in real estate using OPM:

**Seller financing** – Title to the property is transferred to the buyer along with a mortgage or deed of trust and a promissory note that outlines the terms and conditions of the loan the buyer now owes the seller. This strategy may be used instead of providing all the cash needed at closing.

**Subject to existing financing** – When the seller still owes money on the mortgage, the buyer can agree to continue making the seller's mortgage payments in addition to a second payment to the seller to generate profit for the seller.

**Using private money** – This money can be raised from various sources instead of the traditional bank loan. Self-Directed retirement accounts are a popular source used for private money in addition to wealthy investors and hedge funds.

**Hard money** – Generally used for short-term loans and as a last resort. Hard money lenders typically charge higher interest rates and are often for periods of six months to a year. This is a popular strategy for properties that plan to be flipped in a short period of time.

**Working with partners** – You can find investors who are willing to put up the capital while you find the investment and handle the process. Terms of the loans must be negotiated with the silent partners.

But again, keep in mind that with any of these strategies using OPM, most private investors will want to see that you also have some money to contribute towards the investment, assuring that all parties have some "skin in the game".

## 5 THINGS TO FIRST CONSIDER

Step 1: *Educate yourself.*

You can't jump in the ocean before you learn how to swim, and real estate is no different. You can't start investing in real estate before gaining knowledge about becoming a real estate investor. You don't need to go to college and graduate with a degree to educate yourself about real estate. With the developed technological world we live in, you can get everything you need to know with a click of a button. So before buying your first rental property, sit down, bring a hot cup of coffee, and explore the real estate world from the screen of your laptop. Read about the different types of investment properties. Read about the different investment strategies to identify which suits you best. Read about the various financing methods and the aspects of each one. Read about the best locations, return on investments, and previous experiences from past investors. Just read, read, and read about becoming a real estate investor.

Step 2: *Create a plan.*

Probably the most crucial step in becoming a real estate investor is creating a coherent business plan to follow. Having a well-organized plan will save a lot of time and effort when having to make decisions. Include in your plan your investment strategies and your financing strategy, and constantly keep track of your budget. The purpose of writing out a plan is to understand your responsibilities.

After you have completed your research, identify exactly what type of property you are looking to invest in and if it's convenient for you and your budget. Choose the type of income goals you expect from your rental property and identify your ability to maintain the property. Part of your business plan should include deciding how you will be managing the property. Are you going to self-manage the property, or will you hire a professional? Owning a rental property and becoming a real estate investor is a big responsibility, and depending on the type of property you choose, you may need to spend a lot of time acting as a manager. So always have your strategic plan ready!

Step 3: *Choose the right location.*

Real estate investing all boils down to one key factor, which is LOCATION! The location of your investment property will either make you or break you. Therefore, think wisely of the location to ensure that becoming a real estate investor there will be a successful venture.

When searching for the right location, you want to take into consideration whether it will attract tenants. Ask yourself, does the property provide all the public amenities that tenants are searching for? How is the neighborhood? Does it have a low crime rate and a high employment rate? There are many details to focus on in terms of location.

Step 4: *Pick an investment strategy and property type.*

Investing in real estate takes many forms, from very passive involvement to very hands-on. There are two main investment strategies to choose from: either Airbnb rentals or traditional rentals. Airbnb is a type of investment that is "short-term" because you are renting out your property to tenants who only want a property to stay in for a short period of time. Traditional rentals, on the other hand, are long-term.

Not only do you have to choose a strategy but also the type of property you want to invest in. Do you want condos, single-family, multi-family, or apartments? Before becoming a real estate investor, you need to decide on which strategy and property type suit your plan best and make sure they also fit your budget.

Step 5: *Real estate market analysis*

Becoming a real estate investor can be easy and simple by using real estate market analysis. This allows you to determine the best properties to invest in and predict the profitability and value of each real estate investment before you invest in it. The real estate market analysis allows you to compare multiple similar properties based on information about each property to determine what price is most suitable for your investment.

## SPENDING YOUR OWN TIME AND MONEY ON REAL ESTATE INVESTMENTS

Spend some time assessing and prioritizing your plans before you get started. Thinking through your financial, professional, and personal goals is necessary since they will affect how you launch and grow your real estate investing company. Start by considering where you want to be in 5, 10, and 15 years.

- Purchasing and owning real estate is a financial strategy that may be both enjoyable and advantageous. Instead of investing in stocks and bonds, potential real estate owners might utilize leverage to purchase assets by paying a portion of the whole price up front and then paying the remaining balance, plus interest, over time.
- While a traditional loan decades ago would typically demand a 20% down payment, in today's market, a 3% down payment is sufficient for purchasing your first property, depending on your investment strategy. The ability to own the asset as soon as the paperwork is signed empowers landlords and real estate flippers, who can then obtain second mortgages on their homes to pay off the mortgages on additional properties.

When seeking out the best return on your investment, be sure to consider all aspects of the project, including the purchase price, renovation cost, and the after-repair value of the property.

The term "after repair value," or "ARV" in real estate, refers to the estimated value of a property following the completion of all improvements and repairs. This figure is crucial for real estate investors, especially those who flip homes, as it determines the difference between the "as-is" value of the desired investment property and the value of a developed property that has undergone a thorough renovation.

**Current Value of the Property x Cost of Renovations = ARV**

The purchase price plus the total cost of repairs forms the basis of the property's selling price. The fact that repairs pay for themselves more than once is the secret of property flipping's profitability.

As an investor, you will need to be able to obtain precise repair estimates and knowledge of the neighborhood market for the ARV to be correct. Most of the time, seasoned investors with years of experience flipping houses can enter a property, assess it, and swiftly assign a value based on their knowledge and expertise. This won't be the case for less experienced investors, and it will take some time.

The ARV is determined by taking a moment in time and calculating the property's value based on the housing market at the time and the home's condition. Throughout a home's remodeling, this value may fluctuate every day.

Using the after-repair value, you can plan your strategy and choose the finest real estate financing option. Investors can get a decent idea of the selling price of an investment property from the ARV.

**The 70% Rule: What Is It?**

For investors in real estate, this guideline is well-liked. It provides the greatest amount you ought to invest in a house to flip. What's the key to flipping houses successfully? Buying homes at a low enough price so that when you sell them, you make a large profit. Overspending on the front end of a home purchase will make it much more difficult to earn those big dollars.

But how do you determine when a home's sales price is right? The 70% rule can help.

**What Is The 70% Rule In House Flipping?**

Home flippers have a simple plan for earning money: They buy a home cheaply, fix it up, and then sell it at a higher price. The goal for flippers is to buy low and then sell high to boost their profits.

The 70% rule can help flippers when they're scouring real estate listings. Basically, it says that investors should pay no more than 70% of the after-repair value of a property minus the cost of the repairs necessary to renovate the home.

What does this mean? The after-repair value, or ARV, of a property, is the amount that a home could sell for after flippers renovate it. When buying a home to flip, investors need to estimate how much they think the property could sell after it's been renovated. They can then multiply that amount by 70% and subtract it from the estimated cost of renovating the property.

The resulting figure is the highest price that flippers should consider paying for that property.

The key here, though, is to realize that the 70% rule is just a general rule of thumb. Before buying any home, you need to study market conditions, work with real estate professionals to get a more accurate resale estimate, and meet with contractors to determine how much repairs will cost and which renovations are needed.

**How Does The 70% Rule Work?**

The 70% rule relies on a simple calculation:

> **After-repair value (ARV) ✕ .70 − Estimated repair costs = Maximum buying price**

That maximum buying price will give you an idea of how much you should spend on a home that you plan on renovating and reselling. Going above that price could jeopardize your profits.

**Is It A Rule Or A Guideline?**

Though it's known as the 70% rule, this pricing strategy is more of a guideline. The number you get after running the 70% rule might not be the right price to offer a seller. Depending on market conditions, you might need to make a higher offer. If you're buying in a down real estate market, you might be able to purchase your home at a lower cost. The key, as always, is to study market conditions before making any offer.

**Limitations of After Repair Value (ARV)**

Comparable property values might increase or decrease as a result of changes in the housing market, the cost of renovations can vary, and the property itself might have concealed issues, so you always want to allot a contingency fund for the unknowns that may occur.

# CHAPTER 3
# DEVELOPING YOUR MILLIONAIRE CONFIDENCE

If you follow any influencers or pay any attention to social media, you've likely encountered the phrase "millionaire mindset." That is fundamental to hustle culture. Individuals often casually remark about having a millionaire mentality or tell you that you need one, but what does this phrase mean? Is it something that people independently learn?

A millionaire mentality has nothing to do with making a million dollars. It has nothing to do with your net worth, living in a penthouse in New York, real estate, financial security, or bank balance. According to those who swear by it, a millionaire mindset is focusing on transforming your life, beginning with your viewpoint, in order to achieve the goals you've always desired.

That is not a simple task.

Daily encouragement of purposeful behaviors and ways of thinking is required. The concept is that millionaires reside in a place of wealth that affords them greater success and self-assurance. To attain your goals, you must first act as if you have already accomplished them. In that environment, your success drives further success. What are the habits of a millionaire mindset? What is required to have a millionaire's mindset? Here are some "millionaire mindset" practices for you to adopt:

*Focus on your goals.*

How are you going to achieve your objectives if they are not on your mind? Your objectives may include financial growth, enhanced well-being, a specific professional path, or any other desire. Make it a practice to consider your goals regularly. (On average, it takes 66 days to create a habit.) Once you have established your goals, write them down and store them someplace you will see them frequently. They will always be there to remind you of your goals, even on difficult days.

*Get comfortable with always learning.*

Individuals must frequently keep in mind that there is always an opportunity to begin anew in the world. When pursuing objectives, it may be necessary to employ alternative methods.

Adapting to frequent change may help you recognize that your previous techniques were ineffective. Small skills assist as well. Take note of all the new skills you acquire and be pleased with how far you've come.

*Put yourself out there.*

You cannot attain your goals by staying inside your home and avoiding social interaction.

It is crucial to network and pay attention to how you promote yourself. If you are attempting a business pitch, you must exude confidence and enthusiasm. People identify and remember powerful, passionate, and fearless speakers who articulate their objectives. Networking can help you connect with people who share the same motivations as you. Developing friendships at work transforms coworkers into peers, which boosts employee engagement.

*Be Patient.*

It can be discouraging to feel like you're working hard without being rewarded, but this should not dissuade you from pursuing your life goals. You cannot alter your life in one week.

It is acceptable if you fall short of your growth objectives. Good things take time, and the fact that they don't always occur when you want them to does not imply that they never will.

*Accept mistakes as they come.*

Mistakes are necessary for growth and learning. Mistakes should not be viewed as things that must be avoided at all costs, but rather as learning opportunities. Also, keep in mind that there is a distinction between careless errors (which you should avoid) and unsuccessful strategies that provide you with additional knowledge and insight to try a new approach. Failures are opportunities to learn about oneself and one's team, as well as an excellent approach to acquiring new talents for the future. Instead of obsessing over your mistakes, you should reflect on them and accept them as you continue to improve.

*Don't forget about sleep.*

To accomplish our best work, we need to be well-rested. Everyone has hectic days, but catching up on sleep is beneficial for the mind and body. When our to-do list is packed, staying up late and pushing ourselves too hard can be tempting, but this is unsustainable. Even if you believe an additional hour of work will bring you closer to your objectives, it will likely increase your exhaustion and decrease your productivity. Next time this occurs, make a deliberate decision to sleep. A well-rested body and mind will increase your motivation and readiness to begin the day.

*Keep growth in mind.*

Professional and personal development is inevitable as you pursue your goals. Maintaining a growth attitude along your journey to achievement is vital to remind yourself of your beginnings. If you have long-term objectives, take the time to evaluate your progress.

In addition to feeling a sense of success, you will also be more driven. When you're feeling frustrated, splitting your objectives into multiple tasks might make your progress seem more tangible. Growth does not occur overnight or without effort, both of which you have demonstrated. You should treasure the sense of pride that comes from reflecting on your progress.

*Stop making excuses for yourself.*

Excuses will prevent you from moving forward and accomplishing your objectives. Do you have a problem? Use some tried-and-true problem-solving approaches. Instead of blaming your setbacks on other sources or complaining, try to address them. Consult with a dependable coach or mentor to determine what is holding you back or causing the issue. Concentrate on changing your behavior to effect change for yourself. Remember that the worst thing you can do is to allow your excuses to consume you, whether that means asking for assistance, altering your strategy, or even taking a break.

*Learn to invest.*

Regarding financial success, the millionaire's mindset is straightforward: never lose money.

Invest in your future by prioritizing your financial health and establishing financial objectives that emphasize investing over consumption. If you must incur financial risks, such as investment capital, you should be confident that the expenditure will yield a return. Do study and collaborate closely with successful business people, taking their advice to heart.

*Adopt a "now" mentality.*

Although patience is a virtue, one of the habits of affluent individuals is to seize fresh possibilities. There will also be fewer revenue-generating opportunities, such as speaking at events and volunteering to support a business, as a result of these changes. The larger your experiences and connections, the higher your chances of progressing personally and professionally.

Here are 7 pro tips for achieving the millionaire mindset.

1. **Trust in yourself**

The millionaire mindset is not something that can be practiced for three days and then its benefits are enjoyed in perpetuity. It may take longer than anticipated. Trust that you will eventually achieve your goals. Remember that doing your best is all you can ask for when attempting to become the neighbor's billionaire.

2. **Be considerate along the way**

While you undergo this lifestyle adjustment, you will inevitably face frustrating situations and individuals. It is acceptable to be upset or disappointed, but strive to be as respectful as possible. If you achieve your objectives, you will feel more accomplished if you have shown gratitude to everyone who assisted you along the road.

3. **Replace "I can't" with "I will."**

You will not attempt something if you doubt your ability to do it. Self-prophesy success by reminding yourself as often as possible that you will achieve your goals. Repeat this affirmation daily and more frequently in times of doubt. And don't let setbacks dissuade you from achieving your objectives; the path is not linear.

## 4. Never trust luck

Confidence and a stellar professional trajectory are not everything, so always be prepared for unforeseen circumstances. Imagine the worst-case scenarios, develop a plan to cope with them, then work diligently to avoid them. For instance, economic uncertainty might result in financial setbacks such as layoffs or a recession. Save more than your budget dictates to be prepared for any eventuality.

## 5. Think big!

Setting a specific aim and linking each daily task to its advancement can help you stay motivated and comprehend why you're working so hard. When you're feeling stuck or have forgotten your purpose, remind yourself of this vision to spark passion and energy.

## 6. Keep love in mind

While you're working so hard, it's easy to lose sight of what's most important, such as your mental health and relationships. But your well-being is contingent upon your social health.

According to research, strong social relationships are associated with longer life, less stress, and better heart health. Consider your friends, family, and workplace as you pursue your ambitions. They will motivate you, you will inspire them, and this emphasis on love will propel you forward.

## 7. Thinking like a millionaire!

Developing a millionaire's mindset does not happen quickly. It requires vision, enthusiasm, and a tremendous amount of effort. Have patience and insight, understand that setbacks are typical and teach valuable lessons. Confidence and financial independence are attainable if you firmly grasp your objectives and remain focused.

# CHAPTER 4
# MASTERING THE BRRRR STRATEGY

The BRRRR approach is a terrific strategy for real estate investors who are willing and able to put in the work to generate passive income. It is also superior to conventional finance if you intend to buy more than two houses. With the BRRRR approach, you can recover as much capital as feasible from a project.

What does BRRRR stand for?

BRRRR stands for "buy, renovate, rent, refinance, and repeat." It is an abbreviation for the investment cycle of a savvy investor and should be repeated in that sequence. This strategy focuses on acquiring a distressed property at a discount, rehabilitating or flipping it, renting it out, obtaining a cash-out refinance, and investing the proceeds in additional properties. This strategy is suitable for people who have a thorough awareness of the local rental market and renovation expenditures. The BRRRR Method requires time and a learning curve to master, but once mastered, it is a sustainable approach to buying homes quickly and generating passive income.

*How the BRRRR method works:*

When you buy a property, fix it up, improve its value, and then refinance, you're borrowing against the value of the property at its highest. When done correctly, this allows you to recover more of or sometimes all of the money you invested in the property.

*Here's what you need to know.*

The BRRRR method is a powerful, wealth-building real estate investing strategy that's exploded in popularity lately. Although it's been practiced by successful property investors for decades, only recently has BRRRR emerged in mainstream headlines. The main buzz around the BRRRR strategy in real estate boils down to this—you can buy rental properties and build a large income-producing portfolio without running out of money.

Sounds too good to be true, doesn't it? It's not. It's a tried-and-true model that works in any real estate market if you follow the process.

**BUY**

The purchase of a home is undoubtedly the most crucial phase in the BRRRR process. According to an old saying, you make money in real estate when you purchase. Certainly, this holds correctly for the BRRRR plan. The BRRRR technique will not work unless you purchase excellent bargains.

To ensure the success of the BRRRR method, you must purchase a property for less than its market value. Often, you will purchase a distressed property that is in disrepair or has been mishandled by the present owner to qualify for a discount. Consider purchasing REO houses, wholesale real estate deals, or even a hoarder's home!

Realize that your overall investment in the property, including the purchase price, repairs, closing expenses, and carrying costs, is less than or equal to 75% of the property's after-repair worth (ARV).

**BRRRR Formula: Total Investment = ARV x 75%**

For instance, if you run a comparable and determine that a property's ARV would be $100,000, you should not invest more than $75,000 in the transaction.

Example: $75,000 = $100,000 × 75%

If the ARV is $100,000, your total investment should not exceed $75,000.

You may continue to wonder, "*How much should I pay for a BRRRR property?*"

The following formula will assist you in determining the optimum purchase price for your BRRRR analysis:

**Maximum Acquisition Cost = (ARV x 75%) - Repair Price**

See how that works?

Then, if the transaction passes this test, you should evaluate it as a rental property. You must ensure that the property will provide positive cash flow after you refinance and withdraw your initial investment. Using the property's expected ARV as the new purchase price, calculate the deal's financials as a rental property. Ensure the predicted rental income will meet all planned expenses to ensure the property's long-term viability. Rehabilitating a property can be scary for the majority of conventional homebuyers. This is the reason why real estate investors can negotiate transactions for less than market value. We are willing to address issues that other purchasers and property owners are unwilling to address.

**REHAB**

To rent out the house for top dollar, you will need to make repairs. Based on the required work, you may choose to execute the necessary changes yourself or employ a general contractor. Study comparable properties in your market to assess the level of rehabilitation required to achieve the desired rentals. If you are not selling the home, choose finishes that are lasting, cost-effective, and in keeping with regional market trends for nicer rents. Typically, I prioritize my rehabilitation enhancements as follows:

- Safety
- Functionality
- Aesthetics

*Safety:* Is the repair necessary to ensure the safety of the residents or the property itself? These repairs are non-negotiable and must be completed before anyone can move in. Some examples of such repairs include electrical risks, plumbing leaks, and faulty furnaces. Additional safety concerns, such as mold, termites, and fleas, must also be remedied expeditiously. Investing in security features such as floodlights and deadbolts is always a wise decision.

*Functionality:* Currently, is the property dysfunctional?

Will this fix improve the property's functionality?

Will it make the residents' life here easier and more positive?

These may include the repair of a toilet, the unclogging of a drain, the replacement of a broken ceiling fan, and the installation of new equipment. Following the completion of these tasks, the property should be completely functional and inhabitable.

*Aesthetics:* This pertains to the property's visual appeal and cleanliness. Although the property is habitable, you may wish to replace outdated materials with newer ones. New flooring, granite countertops, paint, and cabinet hardware may be included. In general, these types of enhancements will help you to fetch a higher rent and lease up a unit more quickly than without them.

There are two key questions to keep in mind when rehabbing a rental.

1. What do I need to do to make this house livable and functional?

2. What rehab decisions can I make that will add more value than their cost?

If you rehab correctly and make sure you add value when you do, you are pretty much guaranteed to recover your money—and then some. However, unless you buy and hold luxury rentals, these things aren't necessary:

- Granite countertops
- Brazilian hardwood floors
- High-end stainless-steel appliances
- Bay windows
- Skylights
- Hot tubs
- Chandeliers

It's also rarely worth finishing a basement or a garage for a rental. Instead, consider changes like two-tone paint, refinished hardwoods, and new tile. Moreover, the house must be in decent condition.

Everything must be operational. Being a slumlord will harm you and the industry's reputation in the long term. Obviously, your new investment will not be in good condition when you get it.

That's exactly it!

I seek properties in need of extensive renovations on purpose, knowing that other investors will ignore them and the sellers will be more compelled to reduce their prices.

Here are some of the best problems to search for:

- **Roofs** - In most cases, appraisers will recoup the cost of a new roof through an increase in property value.
- **Uncompleted kitchens** - An outdated kitchen is unsightly yet functional. A partially demolished kitchen renders a home unsuitable for financing, making it easier to purchase with cash.
- **Drywall damage** - Drywall damage renders a house ineligible for financing and discourages prospective purchasers. The glad tidings? Repairing drywall is not a very expensive endeavor.
- **Horrible landscape design** - Overgrown vegetation terrifies the opposition but is inexpensive to restore. You don't need a qualified gardener to trim down overgrown landscaping, so a few hundred bucks will go a long way.
- **Outmoded restrooms** - I frequently renovate bathrooms for $3,000 to $5,000. The majority of bathrooms are small; hence, the material and labor costs are inexpensive. This allows your home to compete with much nicer, higher-ARV properties in the neighborhood.
- **Too few bedrooms** - Houses with over 1,200 square feet but fewer than three bedrooms offer simple opportunities to improve value. Adding a third or fourth bedroom allows the property to compete with far more expensive homes, hence raising its ARV.

By focusing on such properties and doing renovations at prices below market value, you can significantly increase the equity in your acquisitions.

## RENT

Banks are reluctant to refinance unoccupied properties, so renting your home comes first. It is essential to do a thorough screening to obtain tenants who will make monthly payments.

But it's also significant from a financial standpoint. Although appraisers should not place too much emphasis on the cleanliness and friendliness of the renter, everyone is human. First impressions are significant. You must tell the tenant before an evaluation.

I usually advise requesting interior evaluations as opposed to drive-bys. With drive-bys, appraisers are more cautious and may unfairly devalue your property.

Write or place a note on the tenant's door with the date and time, and phone the day before to remind them, unless your local laws stipulate otherwise. Renters are not required to be present, but you should request that they tidy up and kennel their dogs if they are absent. One thing to keep in mind with the BRRRR technique is that because you are borrowing more money against your home, your mortgage will normally be slightly more than with the conventional method. This is quite valuable. The capital in a bank account can be used to grow wealth; however, the equity in a property cannot be used for much. The converse of this reasoning is that your cash flow will decrease significantly due to the increased mortgage payment. This implies you must be even more diligent when analyzing rental comparisons to determine the rent you may expect if you purchase a property.

**What is the BRRRR 1% rule?**

The 1% rule is a simple statistic for determining the probability that a property will generate positive cash flow. The 1% rule states that if you can rent a property for 1% of the price you paid for it, it qualifies. This statistic is crucial for BRRRR investors who intend to retain rental properties rather than sell them.

The 1% rule applies if you purchase a property for $100,000 and can rent it out for $1,000.

The rule is followed if you purchase a house for $200,000 and rent it for $2,000.

The 1% rule is not, however, the only criterion applicable to BRRRR investments.

Consider it a preliminary screening process.

While adopting the 1% rule, there are other elements to consider, such as HOA fees and hefty property taxes. In addition, the costlier the property, the less likely it is to adhere to the norm. Not receiving $6,000 in rent for a $600,000 unit does not always make it a bad investment. It just indicates that you should investigate the property's financial situation further to see whether it is a worthwhile investment.

## REFINANCE

Refinancing your property is the step where your property gets appraised for its new and improved value. At this step, you're hoping the appraised value meets or exceeds your projected after-repair value (ARV). You'll want to shop around for lenders who can do a cash-out refinance. Most lenders require a seasoning period for collected rents before allowing a refinance. This just means the rental income must be collected consistently for a seasoning period of three to six months before a lender can use a new appraisal to collateralize the property.

When you refinance, lenders typically lend up to 70 to 80% of the appraised value.

So, let's look at our example again: Let's say after you fix it up, the property appraises for $110,000. A lender may give you 75% of that value, or $82,500, as a new loan on that property. As long as your total investment in the property was less than $82,500, you'll receive your entire investment back!

If you stick to your original total budget of $75,000, you'll walk away with an additional $7,500 in your pocket after the cash-out refinance.

*Amazing!*

## REPEAT

The "repeat" part of the BRRRR cycle is the most fun. Take everything you learned, gained, and improved upon and put it back into action. Work on building systems, too. Systems help you accomplish your objectives by repeating the same process over and over. Systems cut down on mistakes and stress. The more documented your systems are, the less you'll worry about something being missed, overseen, or forgotten about.

*Why "traditional" isn't always best.*

BRRRR is far better than traditional real estate investing since it enables you to recoup the capital you leave behind. Traditionally, a down payment of a portion of the home's value is made while the home's value is lowest. Consider that investors are continuously looking for opportunities. If an investor is effective at their profession, they will pay less for a property than it is worth. The amount of money a bank will lend you is based on the property's buying price.

If you pay $70,000 for a $100,000 home, the bank will lend you a portion of that amount.

This figure is determined by the loan-to-value (LTV) ratio.

If a bank permits an LTV of 80%, the borrower must make a 20% down payment.

Greater LTVs equate to lower investor down payments. When using the conventional approach, this down payment remains in the transaction. Hence, if you buy $70,000 for a home worth $100,000 and make a 25% down payment, you pay $17,500 for the down payment. You will still need funds for rehabilitation. 20% of the home's after-repair value (ARV) is the average rehab budget for houses acquired conventionally (after-repair value). In this instance, that amount would be $20,000. Reducing this cost by fifty percent leaves you with a $10,000 rehabilitation budget. In the end, you will have spent $80,000 on a $100,000 investment property ($70,000 purchase price plus $10,000 in repairs). The glad tidings? You have accumulated $20,000 in equity. The poor report? You spent $27,500 of your hard-earned money to accomplish this. Keeping your down payment as equity hinders your capacity to purchase other properties. Keeping your rehab budget in the property hinders your capacity to purchase further properties and discourages you from investing additional funds to build equity.

The conventional strategy hinders deal flow. Retaining investing cash is essential for locating better offers and developing investments. Investing gurus are actively engaged in the game. With the conventional way, you run out of money far too quickly. If you want to land lucrative agreements, you must be willing, able, and prepared to close. If you are unable to move, someone else will purchase the property before you can. Conventional borrowing methods impede your progress. Lenders require both valuations and inhabitable properties. Many of the nicest houses are in poor condition, which is why they are so inexpensive. Moreover, the old process causes investors to exhaust their funds rapidly, miss out on truly distressed properties, and close slowly. These elements diminish your chances of landing the contract first. The conventional strategy prevents your wealth from expanding. Investing in real estate at a discount to its market value is the best strategy to build wealth.

In the last illustration, you spend $80,000 on a home valued at $100,000.

This increased your net worth by $20,000 before appreciation, loan payoff, and cash flow.

With each standard home purchase, you add $20,000 to your net worth.

Doing so every two months increases your net worth by $120,000.

After slightly more than four years, you would have amassed a million dollars in net worth.

Not bad at all, right? Except that you required $27,500 in cash to increase your net worth by $20,000.

This inhibits you from purchasing additional assets, delays your growth, and restricts other facets of investing, such as receiving the best offers first. If you want to increase your wealth rapidly, effectively, and securely, you must acquire cash-flowing rental properties immediately. Consider purchasing rentals similar to planting trees. Typically, this tree develops, produces more fruit, and increases in value each year. The richest individuals own orchards, not little gardens. Can you cultivate an orchard using conventional techniques? Perhaps, if you have an abundance of cash lying around. Still, it would be slower than with BRRRR.

*Benefits of BRRRR investments*

BRRRR, unlike traditional methods, is meant to win deals rapidly and keep your finances rising.

This is why.

1. Paying less for real estate

In most circumstances, the BRRRR technique will result in a lower purchase price for a property. Pay in cash, or at least without a financing condition. Purchase properties that are not eligible for conventional financing. Quicker and with fewer unforeseen circumstances: Increase the property's value through a renovation so that you can acquire unusual residences at a discount. Suppose you purchase a house for $100,000 in cash and invest $10,000 in repairs. This leaves you with a total investment of $80,000 on a $100,000 property. In the BRRRR approach, the refinance phase follows the rehabilitation phase. The bank values the property at $100,000, not the $70,000 you paid for it. At the same 75% LTV, you could refinance and recoup $75,000 if you chose to do so. Considering that you only spent a total of $80,000 on purchasing and renovating the home, this leaves you with only $5,000 in the transaction.

In contrast, the conventional strategy left $27,500 in the bargain.

The BRRRR technique returns $22,500 that would have been retained in the property if it had been acquired via the conventional method.

That's a significant contrast!

2. ...Or possibly paying nothing at all.

Here's a BRRRR method if you're short on funds for your initial deal:

Use the services of a private or hard money lender for the initial down payment. After successfully rehabilitating, renting, and refinancing the property, you can repay the initial loan and reinvest the proceeds.

3. A high rate of return

A successful BRRRR does not necessitate a significant amount of cash outlay. According to BRRRR, a smaller initial investment results in a greater return on investment. Let's assume you've invested $10,000 in a home, as investment guru Brandon Turner explains here. If it generates $2,500 in annual cash flow, the cash-on-cash return is 25%, and we haven't even begun assessing the built-up equity. Developing equity. Equity is one of the greatest aspects of BRRRR. When you are choosing properties with significant possibilities for renovation, you immediately build equity in the deal. This equity cascades to the following transaction, so increasing your net value.

4. Renting a class-A property

You've invested a lot of money (or physical blood, sweat, and tears) on your property, and you can certainly increase its value. Perhaps it was more class C (or even worse!) when you purchased it, but it is now a class A beauty. This results in better tenants and reduced maintenance costs.

*Is the BRRRR method risky?*

This method maximizes the return on investment for investors. Yet, there are a few risks of BRRRR that you should investigate before diving in. These are some factors to consider.

1. The short-term loan

If you have the funds to finance your initial transaction without involving a lender, this is not a concern. (Let's not overlook the heartfelt congratulations!) Yet, if you require finance, you must examine the loan's fees. How much will your carrying costs be? What kind of rates are available? Keep in mind that private and hard money lenders typically charge higher rates of interest, which can lower your cash flow. Beginning with a home equity loan on an existing property is one choice. This provides you with initial funding without the same degree of danger.

2. Appraisal risks

Refinancing is an essential component of BRRRR; without it, the acronym would simply be BRRR. But refinancing requires a home appraisal, which makes math skills crucial. If you miscalculate the after-repair value and the property does not appraise, it will be difficult to repeat the transaction.

3. Waiting for seasoning

Here's another annoying aspect about refinancing: Numerous conventional and portfolio lenders require that properties "age" beforehand. Seasoning entails waiting between six and twelve months before refinancing. If you are employing a private or hard money lender, it is essential to evaluate the actual cost of this time scale.

4. Rehab pains

You may enjoy the concept of house renovation, but the rehabilitation phase is nothing like HGTV. Ready to juggle absentee contractors, unexpected issues such as asbestos, and a multitude of other difficulties. Rehabilitating is not a deal-breaker, but you shouldn't enter this stage with rose-colored glasses on.

## CHAPTER 5
# HOW TO PAY FOR YOUR BRRRR

If you can pay cash outright, that's always best. But you don't need to have significant savings to start your BRRRR journey. Here are some options to cover purchasing the property and funding the rehab.

1. Use a HELOC

One of the greatest advantages of homeownership is the opportunity to accumulate equity over time. You can leverage equity to access low-cost cash through a second mortgage, either a one-time loan or a home equity line of credit (HELOC). Each of these forms of credit has advantages and disadvantages, so it is essential to be aware of both before moving further.

There may also be further solutions worth examining. As collateral, home equity loans and home equity lines of credit leverage the difference between your house's worth and your mortgage balance. As the loans are secured by the house's equity, home equity loans offer highly attractive interest rates that are typically comparable to those of first mortgages. You will pay less in financing fees for the same loan amount as compared to unsecured sources of credit, such as credit cards. There is, however, a disadvantage to using your property as collateral. Home equity lenders place a second lien on your property, giving them the same rights as the first mortgage lender if you default on your payments. The more you borrow against your property or condominium, the greater your risk.

## How Much Can Be Borrowed With Home Equity Loans?

Second mortgages are underwritten similarly to other house loans. They each have criteria dictating how much they can lend based on the value of the property and the borrower's credit history. This is stated as the combined loan-to-value ratio (CLTV). This ratio compares the value of all secured debts, including first and second mortgages, to the value of the property. This is an illustration.

Suppose you are working with a bank that gives a maximum CLTV ratio of 80%, and the value of your home is $300,000.

If you now owe $150,000 on your first mortgage, you may be eligible for a home equity loan or HELOC of $90,000 ($300,000 x 0.80 = $240,000 - $150,000 = $90,000).

A home equity loan is issued as a lump sum. If you need money for a one-time expense, such as a welding or kitchen renovation, this is an alternative. When you take out one of these loans, you will typically be charged a fixed interest rate, so you know exactly what your monthly payments will be. If you need a modest amount of cash, home equity loans are typically not the best option. While some lenders will provide loans for $10,000, the majority will not provide loans for less than $35,000. In addition, you must pay many of the same closing charges as a first mortgage, including loan processing fees, origination fees, appraisal fees, and recording fees. Lenders may demand you to pay points or interest paid in advance, at closing. Each point corresponds to 1% of the loan amount. Hence, one point on a $100,000 loan would cost $1,000.

Points reduce your interest rate, which could be advantageous in the long term. Yet, if you want to pay off the loan early, the upfront interest is not exactly to your advantage. If you believe this to be the case, you can frequently bargain with your lender for less or even no points.

HELOCs differ from home equity loans in their operation. Like credit cards, they are a revolving source of funds that you can access at your discretion. Most banks provide a variety of methods for accessing account funds, including internet transfers, paper checks, and credit cards linked to the account. In contrast to home equity loans, they typically have little, if any, closing charges and variable interest rates. However, some lenders provide fixed rates for a set number of years. There are advantages and disadvantages to the flexibility offered by credit lines. You can borrow at any moment against your credit line, but unused funds do not accrue interest. As long as your bank does not have a minimum withdrawal requirement, this is a good source of emergency finances. For instance, if you have lost your job, need cash, and have equity in your home, a HELOC may be a viable option. Again, the largest disadvantage is that your property acts as collateral for a HELOC. If for whatever reason, you are unable to repay your HELOC, you risk losing your home to foreclosure.

2. Consider a conventional loan

This method is not optimal for BRRRR, but it is also not impossible. If you already own property, start by talking to your present lender. They can explain the intricacies of funding a renovation with a conventional loan. Keep in mind that conventional loans drastically restrict the types of properties that can be purchased, and BRRRR is most effective when the property has significant issues, such as a faulty roof or HVAC system. In addition, conventional loans close far more slowly, which undermines one of BRRRR's primary advantages.

Underwriting standards can be stricter for rental property applicants. Mortgage lenders focus on credit score, down payment, and debt-to-income ratio, and though the same factors apply to rental property mortgages, the borrower will likely be held to a more stringent credit score, DTI thresholds, and a higher minimum down payment:

- Credit score: A minimum score of 620, with better rates and terms offered with scores of 740 and higher.
- Down payment: 0-3% may be acceptable on a conventional mortgage for a primary residence, but borrowers for investment real estate generally have to plan on 15% to 25% down.

- Debt-to-income ratio (DTI): DTI represents the percentage of the borrower's monthly income that goes toward debt. Lenders will generally allow you to count up to 75% of your expected rental income toward your DTI.6
- Savings: Borrowers should have cash available to cover three to six months of mortgage payments, including principal, interest, taxes, and insurance.

3. Use hard money or a private lender.

The ideal hard money lender will finance up to 90% of the acquisition price and 100% of the development costs. And when you make a purchase, they are treated like cash, which helps you remain competitive. However, certain private or hard money lenders will need an appraisal, reducing your competitive advantage. In addition, they will pay particular attention to possible rents and may have minimum income restrictions. And then there is the greatest disadvantage: rates. They are often significantly more than a conventional mortgage, so you should carefully calculate your holding costs.

*Refinancing your BRRRR*

Assuming you've completed the renovation and rented out the property, it's time to refinance. Arrange your refinancing before you purchase. Consider it too late, and you may be forced to scramble for an acceptable solution. Two primary refinancing options exist.

1. Conventional financing

This is the most prevalent option available to BRRRR investors. It entails working with a conventional lender to obtain a Fannie Mae or Freddie Mac-backed mortgage. (But you should seek out lenders who are acquainted with investors.) These loans may have loan-to-value ratios of up to 75%. These loans often include the lowest interest rates and costs, as well as no prepayment penalties. Nonetheless, conventional lenders frequently have stringent underwriting restrictions; therefore, you should review the requirements before purchasing the home to avoid unpleasant surprises.

2. Commercial financing

Commercial financing is an excellent option for investors. It entails underwriting the property as a rental property and allows for a maximum loan-to-value of 80%. Unlike conventional financing, these loans feature higher interest rates and prepayment penalties, and you may be required to personally guarantee the transaction. Consider searching for business lenders who offer both commercial and rehab loans. This saves money and time.

*How to become a black belt investor?*

The good news is that if you adhere to the concepts that lead to a good BRRRR bargain, you will surely adhere to the same ideas that lead to successful real estate investing. By understanding the five elements of BRRRR, you will also master the process of accumulating wealth via real estate. A martial artist with a black belt practices specific motions, maneuvers, and techniques until they can execute them flawlessly. When investors undertake the same action repeatedly, they can reach a point where they can execute it at a very high degree. Via BRRRR, you recover a greater proportion of your capital, allowing you to purchase more deals and increase your net worth more quickly.

Get a black belt in investing by conducting more transactions, which:

Establishes within the community the reputation as a person who can close. This suggests that more opportunities will come your way.

Enhances your knowledge, making you smarter, quicker, and better. Contractors will offer you greater rates on your renovation projects if you can increase their profits.

Allows you to pay less in property management fees as a result of a larger portfolio.

Allows you to earn additional money by wholesaling, flipping, or selling your homes to other investors, turnkey-style.

Increases leverage with local banks to obtain more favorable funding arrangements.

There is a value in quantity. To become a black belt investor, more repetition and practice are required. This is considerably easier if you utilize the BRRRR approach and your capacity to build riches by recuperating more funds and purchasing additional real estate. BRRRR investing is the most effective method of real estate investment.

I frequently advise investors not to purchase anything unless they can BRRRR. It will have a significant impact on your financial well-being and alter the way you invest.

## CHAPTER 6

# BUILDING WEALTH THROUGH REAL ESTATE

It's a common misconception that you must be either wealthy or a real estate expert to invest in real estate. The reality is that everybody can participate in real estate in some capacity, even if they have a small initial investment capital. Real estate is an excellent portfolio diversifier. Whether they invest directly or indirectly in real estate, real estate investors earn substantial returns on their investments.

*What Does It Mean to Invest in Real Estate?*

Investing in real estate can refer to a variety of activities. It indicates that you purchase a home, add a household to it, and rent it out to renters. In addition to the appreciation of the residence, you can earn monthly cash flow through rent payments. There are other additional options to invest in real estate, which will be discussed below. Generally, it indicates that you invest in real estate via equity (property ownership) or debt (loaning the funds to buy the property). Regardless of how you invest in real estate, you may receive monthly cash flow, capital gains through appreciation, or loan interest. When you invest in real estate, you diversify your portfolio, so you aren't reliant on the pitiful savings account rates banks offer today or putting all of your money in danger in the stock market, which we all know can collapse in an instant.

## Who Qualifies to Invest in Real Estate?

You don't need to be an accredited investor to invest in real estate. Numerous individuals incorrectly believe this and avoid real estate until they have more money or experience. You do not require it, however. One can invest in real estate if they have the desire and a modest amount of capital. If you wish to invest in physical real estate (i.e., own the property), a down payment is required. Nonetheless, if you have good credit and a low debt-to-income ratio, you can borrow the remainder, allowing you to leverage your investment significantly more than any other investment. If you do not wish to own real estate, you only need to meet the minimum investment criterion, which is typically less than $1,000, to qualify.

## What Are the Benefits of Investing in Real Estate?

As with any investment, there are benefits and cons to real estate. There are risks, but if there were no risks, there would be no rewards, right? When you have ample assistance, you may enjoy the rewards of real estate investing without being overly concerned about the associated risk. Here are the leading advantages of real estate investment:

*Cash flow* - You may earn cash flow if you purchase and hold real estate or invest in the equity of a property (REIT). In the case of buying and keeping real estate, the rent will generate monthly cash flow. After paying the mortgage and property expenses, the remaining balance is yours. This is an excellent way to save for future investment, a rainy day, or to boost your retirement income.

*Financial security* - Real estate appreciates naturally. There are instances when values decline, but the market typically recovers. If you are in it for the long haul, you will likely experience significant appreciation, which will result in bigger earnings upon sale. Several individuals utilize real estate investments as their long-term retirement strategy. They anticipate selling the property during retirement for a profit and using the proceeds to supplement their retirement income.

*Tax advantages* - If you invest in real estate to purchase, hold, and rent it out, you can deduct your expenses just like a business owner. Although it is an investment, it is also a business. By owning a property and enjoying its value and cash flow, you will reduce your tax liability and boost your profits. While investing in stocks and bonds, you have no control. You only have a say in the purchase and sale of the asset. When you invest in a company, your earnings and investment possibilities are dependent on that company. But when you invest in real estate, you are in charge. You have control over the rents, the length of time you hold the property, and you can even induce appreciation by making renovations.

*Top 5 Ways to Build Wealth Through Real Estate*

1. Acquire Rental Properties

There are several ways to purchase rental homes. You can purchase them from a real estate agent using the MLS system or a property that is for sale by the owner. You negotiate the purchase price, close on the home, then market the property to attract tenants. You can also employ a service to purchase a turnkey or tenant-occupied property. After purchasing a home, you will eliminate the preceding processes. It's like if you were an instant landlord; you own the property and renters are already residing there.

2. Fix and Flip Homes

If you are a fan of reconstructed shoes, you may want to attempt flipping residences. You will need a keen eye for detail to identify undervalued properties. The fix-and-flip strategy only works when a home is available for less than its prospective value. You purchase the property, renovate it, and resell it for a substantial profit, pocketing the proceeds. To purchase fix-and-flip properties, you must have the funds or finance to purchase and renovate the property.

You also need a large network of professionals to assist you in locating the property, completing the improvements, and pricing the home for sale.

3. Wholesaling

Consider wholesaling if you do not wish to take possession of a property and have an enormous network of investors on your side.

Wholesalers do not purchase the properties but rather seek them out, locating discounts in various regions. When they discover an opportunity, they submit an offer and sign a contract. Wholesalers make two types of real estate investments:

Purchase the property and sell it immediately — Wholesalers with enough funds to buy a home in cash will purchase it at the undervalued price they agreed and then sell it to an investor in their network for a profit. The transactions occur within a week of one another, so the wholesaler does not leave a large amount of money on the table for an extended period.

Conduct a double closure - Some wholesalers do not purchase the property in person. Instead, they enter into a contract to purchase the property with the seller and a deal with a higher-priced buyer. Both deals finalize simultaneously at the title business, with the investor (the final purchaser) paying the original seller with funds from his purchase. The wholesaler maintains his position as the middleman and profits from the difference between the final selling price and the price he negotiated with the seller.

4. Investment in real estate investment trusts

If you are not prepared to invest in tangible real estate, you can invest in REITs. This is a wonderful alternative for novices because you may invest with small sum, and you have no obligations. The majority of investors begin with REITs or income-producing properties.

A REIT is comparable to purchasing property shares. You receive dividends based on the income generated by the property. REITs typically offer greater dividends than ordinary stocks and are a fantastic way to diversify a stock portfolio and/or get started in real estate investing. Some investors participate in debt real estate investment trusts. Debt REITs invest in the money loaned to investors for the purchase of properties; hence, they do not provide the same dividends. You will earn a fixed interest rate and have a predetermined date to repay the principal.

5. Real Estate Crowdfunding

You have probably encountered crowdfunding platforms by now. They combine the funds of all investors to invest in a huge project, in this case, real estate. But, similar to investing in tangible real estate, this might be dangerous. Before investing in crowdsourcing, you should conduct a thorough study. Know the recipient of the funds and their track record in constructing, maintaining, and managing investment properties. Verify the investor is knowledgeable and has successfully managed investments in the past; otherwise, you risk losing your cash.

The key to selecting the ideal real estate investment is to consider your budget, objectives, and risk tolerance.

Ask yourself:

o   How much capital must I invest?

- Do I have sufficient credit to qualify for another mortgage?
- Am I willing to assume the risks associated with property ownership, including maintenance, financing, and finding/retaining tenants?
- Would I prefer a less hazardous investment that buys larger real estate holdings with other investors?
- Am I attempting to diversify my portfolio of investments, or is this my first investment?

You'll determine what's right for you when you do a little soul-searching. Investing in real estate can be a great way to make monthly cash flow, earn appreciation, and set yourself up to meet future goals.

## CHAPTER 7
# WHOLESALING THE "QUICK CHECK"

Real estate investing is unlike investing in stocks and bonds. With the latter two, depending on the type of investment, you may be able to dive right in with perhaps as little as $100. You may leave whenever you choose. When dealing with real estate, things are not so simple. In truth, real estate transactions can be difficult to negotiate and are frequently expensive. Also, it takes time to purchase and sell a home. First, there is the matter of the initial deposit. You also need additional finance to cover any costs that your down payment does not cover. You must complete an abundance of papers. Then there is the closing, not to mention the time necessary to manage renters and collect rent. You have options if you want to invest in real estate but can't stomach the notion of all the money needed and the acquisition procedure. Real estate wholesale is one of them. It is a legal approach for purchasing real estate without committing to the purchase or making a down payment.

Wholesale real estate refers to a short-term business strategy that investors can use to make a quick and steady income in the real estate market. In wholesale real estate transactions, the wholesaler enters into a purchase contract for a home from a seller, for a small earnest money deposit. The contract spells out the amount the wholesaler will sell the property for and the required time for the sale.

After the wholesale real estate deal has been executed, the wholesaler searches for an investor with an interest in the transaction. Once located, the contract is reassigned to the investor for an agreed-upon premium. The price difference is referred to as the wholesale fee, and it can range from 5 to 10 percent of the property's price. This is for the distributor. Often, wholesalers choose distressed properties where the owner is unwilling to invest time or money. Typically, the owner is keen to sell and does not wish to work with a real estate agent. Wholesale real estate may be suitable for those who are interested in real estate transactions but lack the financial means to purchase and sell properties. Often, a real estate license is not required to become a wholesaler (but check your local laws to be sure). If you are sociable and hardworking, wholesale real estate may be a good fit for you.

*How to Wholesale Property*

Real estate wholesaling does not require a significant amount of capital, but it does require a wholesaler to conduct the appropriate property research, network to identify suitable investors, and design a financial agreement that the investor will accept.

The steps involved in real estate wholesaling are shown below.

1. Conduct Research

Discover the wholesale legislation in your jurisdiction. Moreover, investigate the areas and neighborhoods where you intend to purchase the property.

2. Identify distressed properties

Search for properties that are underpriced and whose owners are motivated to sell. The owners of foreclosed or lien-encumbered properties may be willing to sell for less than market value. Several resources could assist you in locating such properties:

- Multiple Listing Service (MLS)
- Networking organizations and online property auction websites
- Social networking sites
- Foreclosure sites

3. Do the Math and Due Diligence

Once you have located a property that meets your criteria, you must ensure that your wholesale real estate deal will be profitable. First, determine the property's current market value. Comparing sold properties in the neighborhood, occupancy rates, and cash-on-cash returns can be helpful. Determine the cost of any necessary repairs next. This data will help you to compute the value after repairs (the fair market value after repair is done). This allows you to compute the maximum acceptable offer (the highest price you can offer for the distressed property and still make a profit).

4. Contact the seller

Describe your job as a real estate wholesaler and how working together to sell their property may be an effective strategy. Specify how the wholesale real estate deal would be conducted. As long as state rules are obeyed, wholesale real estate transactions are legal, and there is nothing to hide.

5. Obtain a Property Contract

Make your offer to the seller and enter into a contract for the property. Ensure that your contract allows for the assignment of the contract to another party. Include in your contract a clause that allows you to withdraw from the arrangement if you are unable to find a buyer before the contract's expiration. This decreases your risk.

6. Locate a cash buyer

After locating the ideal property and negotiating a wholesale real estate contract with the seller, you must market your contract to prospective cash buyers. Utilize your offline and online networking talents to contact possible investors. You might also contact nearby real estate agents and inquire about previous cash acquisitions.

7. Reassign the Agreement to the Buyer

It is the moment to finalize the transaction with the investor that best complements your wholesale real estate purchase. You must both agree to the terms and conditions. Obviously, as a real estate distributor, you want to get compensated for the time you spent locating the distressed property and closing the deal.

*Pros and Cons of Wholesale Real Estate*

**Pros**

Real estate wholesaling may educate you on the real estate market and hone your negotiation abilities. It is a low-risk method of producing money because it involves a small initial investment. In most cases, a portion of the fee is paid upon assignment of the purchase agreement and the remainder upon the closure of the property transaction. No credit score, positive or negative, is required. There is no requirement for renovation experience or effort. If you have a strong investor network, you can sell the house quickly. Depending on the number of deals you play, you may earn a substantial profit in a short amount of time.

**Cons**

To earn a steady income rapidly, you must build (or already possess) superior networking skills and a solid pipeline of prospective investors. In reality, you won't earn any money until you identify properties and investors, so a significant amount of sweat equity may be necessary while you perfect the process and build your book. In some states, a real estate license is required to wholesale property. The profit margin on wholesale real estate deals is lower than that of other real estate ventures. Due to the dependence on suitable/available characteristics, they can be erratic. If wholesalers are unable to obtain investors, their earnest money deposits may be forfeited. Property owners can be unfamiliar with or uncomfortable with the wholesale real estate strategy.

*How to Succeed at Real Estate Wholesale*

Wholesale real estate is not for everyone. It involves considerable effort, time, dedication, and perseverance. Also, you must have excellent communication and marketing skills. You must construct a network of investors who may be interested in purchasing the properties you discover. Locating the right property type is one of the keys to wholesale success. Owners of troubled homes who are willing to sell are excellent prospects.

This is the type of real estate that can attract potential investors. Before submitting an offer to the seller, you should examine the types of repairs and improvements the home will require. These are some characteristics that can help an individual become a successful real estate wholesaler:

- A mindset that is goal-oriented and committed to accomplishing objectives.
- The capacity to arrange and approach things effectively.
- Ability to delegate responsibilities when it is beneficial.

- A realization is that collaborating with individuals who have access to potential leads, such as the Multiple Listing Service, can be necessary.
- A fondness for technology (such as customer relationship management software and mobile applications) that can streamline and improve the overall wholesale real estate business.
- A comprehension of the effectiveness and importance of a well-designed website for marketing services and disseminating vital information to prospective sellers and investors.
- A willingness to learn more with each wholesale transaction and to ensure that both the seller and the buyer are satisfied with the wholesale real estate deal.

Real estate wholesaling may sound complicated, but it's actually very simple.

Let's say a homeowner has a property they don't believe could sell because it's fairly distressed. The owner doesn't have the resources to fix it up and just continues to live in it, thinking they'll never get a fair price for it. Enter the wholesaler, who approaches the homeowner with an offer. Together, they agreed to put the house under contract for a purchase price of $90,000. Using a network of investors, the wholesaler finds an eager buyer at $100,000.

The wholesaler assigns the contract to this investor, who then has a profitable fixer-upper project. The wholesaler makes a $10,000 profit without having to buy the home. Essentially, the wholesaler contracted with the homeowner to find an interested party to buy the house. Under the contract, the buyer paid $10,000 to the wholesaler and then closed on the purchase with a payment of $90,000.

Wholesale real estate is comparable to flipping. Both use real estate as a tool for investment and profit. Both involve a contract and a home sale. Yet, the time frame for wholesaling is far shorter than that for flipping. In addition, the wholesaler does not undertake any repairs or alterations to the property. Real estate wholesaling is substantially less dangerous than flipping because the wholesaler never really purchases a home. Renovation and carrying costs, such as a mortgage, property taxes, and insurance, are sometimes incurred while flipping a home. Wholesale real estate takes significantly less capital than flipping. Generally, earnest money deposits on a few properties are sufficient. For speedy sales, the wholesaler's success depends on market knowledge and connections with investors.

## CHAPTER 8
## FIX & FLIP THE "FAT CHECK"

Does the thought of taking a broken-down property, fixing it, and selling it to a family looking for their dream home excite you? There are numerous benefits to operating a real estate fix-and-flip business. This includes the one-of-a-kind opportunity to receive satisfaction from renovating a property and the enormous profit possibilities of a fix-and-flip transaction. That does not imply that a fix-and-flip transaction is risk-free. The easiest method to mitigate these dangers is to expand your knowledge of the fix-and-flip procedure.

Fix-and-flip, often known as house flipping, is the practice of purchasing a property that needs repair at a bargain, repairing it, and selling it for a profit within a short time. Bear in mind that if a property is purchased at its full buying price, the resulting profit upon sale will be substantially smaller. To avoid having their cash immobilized and incurring additional expenditures (property taxes, interest rates, etc.), investors must rapidly resell the building. In most perfect situations, a home is purchased, repaired, and sold within a year. Fix-and-flip investments are one of the most popular areas in real estate investing, especially for newcomers, due to their simplicity and low entry barriers.

*How to Fix and Flip a Property in 8 Steps*

Step 1: Research

The first step to a successful fix and flip, as well as any successful real estate deal, is researching everything about the market of the community. If you're interested in doing a fix and flip, be ready to find an answer to any questions you may have about the fix and flip process.

Investors should:

For fix-and-flip investors to be successful, they must understand the local real estate market. Be able to spot a good deal and estimate the property's resale value after renovation. Consider the standard length of time it takes to sell a home in the neighborhood when establishing a timeline. Comprehend the renovation procedure, including prices, local regulations for permits and zoning, project duration, etc. Have a strong team on their side, including a dependable contractor and a competent real estate agent. This research, assuming you do not already have a comprehensive business plan (including a marketing plan), includes a record of your expectations and costs throughout the fix-and-flip process, which is also helpful for bookkeeping and taxes.

A business plan for a fix-and-flip enterprise should have the following components:

- A summary that provides an overview of your project and organization.

- The business opportunity that your company intends to pursue, including the difficulties you've identified in your local market and how you intend to solve them.
- A comprehensive description of your target audience
- A detailed discussion of your company's plan to capitalize on the opportunity.
- A marketing and sales strategy that describes how you want to appeal to your target market.
- A part describing how your firm operates, including vendors, logistics, and technology.
- The project's data and milestones, including expected dates, expenses, and metrics.
- A group demonstration
- A summary of the legal and organizational framework of your company
- A financial plan containing the information necessary for investors to evaluate the performance and viability of your project.

Step 2: Find A Property

You can find a property using a real estate agent to help you find a property. Or you can do the searching yourself by looking for, For Sale By Owners (FSBO) or Distressed or Abandoned Properties.

Either way, ensure that you examine the factors of a property. Think about and determine:

- The risks with the property
- The benefits of the property
- The location
- Its after repair value, or ARV
- Comps
- walk through the property to identify work

Step 3: Obtain Financing

You can invest in real estate even if you have limited funds. How do you intend to pay for the property? This can be accomplished by obtaining a conventional mortgage — and getting pre-approved for a specified amount — and alerting your network of private money lenders that you are using their services.

*Fix and Flip Loan Options #1: Traditional Loans*

The majority of traditional money lenders (banks, credit unions, etc.) are hesitant to give mortgages for fix-and-flip properties since they are viewed as riskier than primary residences. Traditional loan approval is more likely for seasoned investors than for novices. But you may be eligible for a loan if you intend to reside in the house throughout renovations. Keep in mind, if you are a novice real estate investor, that seriously damaged houses, which constitute a substantial portion of potential fix-and-flip properties, do not qualify for traditional loans anyway.

*Fix and Flip Loan Options #2: Private Money*

The majority of investors rely on private money lenders to get fix-and-flip loans. This sort of financing is better suitable for fix-and-flip houses because it is simpler and quicker for investors to secure. Bear in mind that interest rates on alternative mortgages are often substantially higher than those on conventional mortgages.

*Fix and Flip Loan Options #3: Alternative Methods*

If an investor is unable to acquire a loan through conventional or private lenders, there are other choices available. This may involve crowdsourcing or utilizing the equity in other properties (such as their primary property) to secure a home equity loan or a home equity line of credit (HELOC). Whatever the financing method you pick as a real estate investor, you must secure a loan before agreeing to purchase a home. This not only ensures that you have the funds available when you select an investment property, but it also determines the first line of your entire investment budget.

*Step 4: Create a Scope of Work*

The next step is to create a scope of work, which is the roadmap and foundation of your rehab. The scope of work is the outline of work that your contractors will bid and agree on, and it defines what gets done.

As you're doing the scope of work and deciding what you will fix, ask yourself these 4 important questions:

- Will it add value?
- Will it help sell?
- Is it cost-effective?
- Is it needed?

*Step 5: Find the Right Contractor*

Next, it is essential to locate the ideal contractor. Simply said, you should not hire the lowest-priced contractor. Select one that you believe will fulfill the request precisely. Although time is important in fix-and-flip projects, investor-friendly contractors must be responsive from the outset. They should be able to present a portfolio of previous work, preferably on projects comparable to yours. Finally, request references from other investors and contact them to determine whether the contractor followed the following:

Deadlines, finances, the general quality of their work, and more

If you lack familiarity with contractors, you can locate them by:

- Better Business Bureau
- Angie's list
- Craigslist

In this step, you must also determine who will handle the project. This may be because you are aware of the necessary tasks. But this can be time-consuming, detracting from other projects you may be pursuing, such as seeking another property to flip. Also, ensure that you have the proper permits before beginning renovations.

## Step 6: Renovating the Property

The biggest hurdle with property renovation is not going over your budget. During this phase, you can choose to be active or hands-off. While you should work with a designer who will create the plan for the look and layout of the investment property, the actual contracting work should be left to the professionals. Keep an eye on progress because every day that goes by is a day you aren't making money on your fix and flip property, so you should stay updated on the contractor's progress while letting them do their jobs. The most important aspect of this step is to ensure that the progress stays on time and does not go over budget.

## Step 7: Stage & Sell The Property

After the contractor has completed work and renovations are complete, the following step is to put the house on the market; however, to attract buyers, staging is required. It is essential to have it professionally cleaned and staged. Remember that smartphone images cannot compete with high-quality, professional photographs. The ultimate objective of a fix-and-flip is to sell a house for a profit. This favorable return on your fix-and-flip investment enables you to purchase another property after the sale of the first. Let your real estate agent promote the property and provide you with offers from interested parties. After locating a suitable offer, it is time to debrief and repeat the procedure.

**Advantages of Fix and Flip**

A fix-and-flip deal has several advantages; if done the right way. Here are a few of those advantages.

- Funds Are Tied Up For a Short Amount of Time: Unlike other forms of real estate investments, with house flipping, funds are only tied up for a short time. Investors can make a significant profit within months instead of waiting for several years, even decades, to recoup their initial investment.
- Fix and flip houses are significantly more liquid than other real estate assets.
- Excellent Way To Begin Real Estate Investing: Fix and flip deals are an excellent way to dive into real estate investing.
- Although fix and flip has a learning curve, it is also a great way to get a full education in all aspects of real estate. As an investor, you can learn:
    - How to recognize a good deal in your local market
    - The home buying and selling process
    - To establish a professional network including real estate agents, contractors, loan officers
    - To examine firsthand if this is the type of real estate niche you want to specialize in

- **Deal Flexibility:** The process of a fix and flip deal can also offer flexibility depending on your:

  - budget
  - experience
  - priorities

Some investors who have the right experience adopt a hands-on approach, doing most of the work themselves to save money. Meanwhile, others may choose to hire contractors and let them focus on the day-to-day activities while the investor puts his or her attention elsewhere.

**Disadvantages of Fix and Flip**

There are several disadvantages of the fix-and-flip real estate method, including:

*Budget Overruns*

The success of a fix-and-flip deal often depends on a few elements out of the investors' control. For example, renovations may take longer and be more expensive than initially planned if any unexpected defects are discovered while construction is underway.

*Subject to Market Trends*

If the real estate market is sluggish or experiencing a downturn, reselling the property can take longer, and profits may be lower than what you hoped for. In the worst-case scenario, you could end up losing money on your fix-and-flip project.

*Less Tax Advantages*

Owning real estate offers several tax advantages. But for these advantages to be realized, you, the investor, must own them, such as a rental property. When a fix-and-flip deal is complete, the house is sold, and you move on to the next project, voiding the ability to experience tax advantages.

*Time-Consuming*

A fix and flip can be time-consuming. Even if you hire a general contractor to renovate the property, you must supervise the project. Since time is of the essence, every mistake and delay can have serious consequences on your profits. Finally, a house flip does not have the same tax advantages as real estate assets held for a longer time.

**Mistakes to Avoid With Fix and Flip**

Here are some of the most common mistakes associated with house flipping.

*Flipping Mistake #1: Not knowing the local real estate market*

For a profitable fix and flip project, you, as a real estate investor, need to be able to recognize a property priced significantly under market value and evaluate how much you can sell it for once you have fixed it, using tools like after-repair value.

To do so, you need to be extremely aware of:

- the local trends
- what buyers are looking for and their expectations
- and more

*Flipping Mistake #2: Over-improving the property*

Remember: you aren't renovating a house for your needs; you're renovating a house to sell it. By overspending on high-end finishes, you will have issues recouping your costs and selling the property at an acceptable price once all is said and done.

*Flipping Mistake #3: Taking on a project too difficult for your experience level*

Fixing a property can quickly feel like opening Pandora's box. Even though the price of a distressed property may be right, you need to take an honest look at your qualifications and your budget before taking on more than you can chew. If the numbers don't add up, for example, if the profit margins are too low, if it's too much of a risk, or if you already have your hands full with other aspects of your real estate business at the moment, it's important to know when to choose a different property; this is a skill some of the best real estate investors have mastered.

*Flipping Mistake #4: Failure to Write a Business Plan*

When you are trying to make money from a find and flip property, you must have a written business plan to serve as your guideline. Flipping a house can be a lucrative investment, but it's crucial that you have a written plan about how to flip a house. You don't want to be making decisions on the fly, and a business plan ensures that you're not. When you have a written plan that covers costs, marketing, contractors, and every other aspect of your find and flip, you are far less likely to waste money by responding to issues instead of being proactive. The surest way to make a profit flipping houses is to start with a business plan.

*Flipping Mistake #5: Overpricing the Home*

Ultimately, the realtor that you choose to work with when you're ready to sell your find and flip property can only advise you on how much to list the property for.

The ultimate pricing decision is yours. However, you must not become so personally attached to the property that you overprice it when it's completed.

During your time working on the fix and flip, you will see how much the property has improved. It's easy to become sentimental and overvalue the property. Make sure that you're listening to the realtor who provides comparable sales within the given area.

If you overprice the home, your find and flip project will take much longer to sell — and eat into your potential profit.

## CHAPTER 9

# BUY & HOLD THE "FOREVER CHECK"

The buy-and-hold strategy is when an investor buys rental properties that have a good chance of giving them multiple long-term benefits and then keeps them for a long time. To use this kind of strategy, you need to know a lot about the market and how real estate prices change. You would want to know how the market moves so you can buy investment properties when the prices are low and make more money. Also, you can keep an eye on how much your property is worth, so you know when to sell. A good real estate market analysis will also help you figure out how easy it is to sell an asset, which affects how much money you can make from it. The amount of money you could make depends on how marketable each asset is. Your earning potential goes up as your property becomes more marketable.

**Income Sources**

You can choose between two ways to make money from the property you bought:

*Assets grow in value.*

You can choose to keep the property, take care of it, and wait until its value goes up before selling it. But some investors decide to keep the property even if its market value is high.

*Rental*

You can rent out the property to make money, and at the same time, the value of the property will go up.

**Advantages of the "buy and hold" strategy.**

Real estate prices may go up and down because of different things, but they always go back up again. With the "buy and hold" strategy, you can build your wealth over time. In particular, investors who use the "buy and hold" method can take advantage of the following:

- No experience is required.

A good way to start investing in real estate is to buy and hold. You don't need to be an expert or have a lot of experience to buy real estate, and there are many ways to pay for it, such as all-cash, hard money loans, conventional loans, and more. You just need to be ready and willing to learn how things work. It shouldn't be hard to learn how to invest in real estate because there are tools that are easy to use and reliable.

- Short-term gains come quickly.

Let's say the house you bought doesn't need any repairs or fixes. In that case, you can rent it out right away and turn it into a property that brings in regular income.

- The real estate investment portfolio is easy to grow.

The only way to get rich is to wait for the value of your property to go up. Let's say you've paid off the loan on your first home. You can now save the money from your first property so that you can use it as a down payment on a second property in the future. When you have income from two properties, it will be easier to pay the monthly mortgage and buy another property. As you add properties to your portfolio of real estate investments, it becomes easier to look for more properties, and the risks become easier to handle.

- Flexibility.

You can choose how to use a buy-and-hold strategy if you want to make money from it. As we've already talked about, you can choose between two ways to make money. If you don't think you have what it takes to be a landlord, you can choose to make money from the value of your assets going up. On the other hand, if you want to grow your real estate investments more quickly, you can rent out your property and then buy more investment properties.

- More peace of mind.

Even though investing in real estate comes with risks, a "buy and hold" strategy is less volatile, and therefore, has fewer risks. Also, the cash flow is more certain.

- Reduce task responsibility.

When you buy a rental property to keep as an investment, you can deduct costs like repairs and maintenance, property management fees, and even the cost of gas to get to and from your property. The property is also taxed as a lower-taxed investment income.

If you've owned the property for more than a year before you sell it, the long-term capital gains rate will be used to figure out your taxes.

**Drawbacks of the Buy and Hold Strategy**

The buy-and-hold strategy has its problems, just like any other way to invest.

Here are a few examples:

- Risks of Vacancy.

If you own a rental property, you have to look for tenants. Whether you do it yourself or use property management services, finding a tenant could cost you money. If you don't find a tenant quickly enough, your property might sit empty for a while. In that case, you'll have to get the money for your monthly mortgage payment from somewhere else, unless you saved up for a few months' worth of payments before you bought the house.

- Management-intensive.

Investors who aren't good at managing and running things shouldn't buy and keep a rental property. The strategy can be too stressful for investors, especially new ones who don't know much about what it takes to be a landlord. If you want your income property to keep bringing in money, you need to take care of the paperwork and legal issues.

- Illiquidity.

The buy-and-hold plan won't work for investors who want to sell their properties right away for cash. It will take some time for the property's value to go up. You can rent it out right away, but it may take some time to find a good tenant and go through the screening process.

- Chances of losing.

If you decide to rent out your home, you could lose money if there are vacancies or if you get a tenant who doesn't pay the rent. If a renter doesn't pay, you also have to deal with the eviction process, which can be another stressful event.

- Maintenance costs.

Costs keep coming up when you buy and keep the property. Some of these costs are property taxes, electrical system repairs, maintenance of the grounds, plumbing, roofing, and more. As the owner, it will be your job to fix any damage to the property.

- Commitment-dependent.

When you buy and hold, it can take a very long time to reach your investment goals. So, the buy-and-hold strategy might not be for you if you are just testing the water to see if you want to invest in real estate.

- Not what I expected for my money.

Your property may not go up in value as much as you thought it would. Even though you will still make money from it, you may not make as much as you thought you would. This is why you need to do a thorough marketing analysis.

## *Types of Buy and Hold Properties*

A key element of a successful "buy and hold" strategy is the type of property you buy. Especially for new investors, single-family homes are the best buy-and-hold investments. Some investors still only buy single-family homes, even though more experienced investors might be interested in other types of properties. Below is an outline of the two most common types of property and why they make good buy-and-hold investments.

*Single Family Homes*

Single-family homes are houses or condos that stand alone on their lot and can only be rented to one person at a time. They are perfect for first-time investors in real estate who want to buy and hold.

Single-family homes are appealing to investors because of the following:

- Affordability.

Since they are cheaper, you will need less cash even if you buy them in cash.

- Return on investment right away.

After you fix up the place and rent it out, you can start making money right away.

- Regular passive income.

At most, tenants move out once a year. This means that it takes less time and work to find new tenants and hand over the property to them. Single-family homes are also easier to rent out, so you can almost always be sure of getting money from them.

*Multi-Family Homes*

A single-building property built to accommodate more than one family living separately is referred to as a multi-family home. Multi-family residences include duplexes, triplexes, and quadruples, which may be suitable for a buy-and-hold strategy.

Due to the following factors, some investors prefer this kind of property:

- Financing is simpler.

While multi-family homes may cost more, banks and other financing organizations are more likely to grant loans for this kind of real estate. This is because multi-family properties produce a sizable amount of monthly cash flow.

- Faster to create a portfolio.

Those who are eager to expand their real estate investment portfolio would be wise to buy a multi-family property. Buying a multi-home allows you 2 to 4 investment properties right away, unlike buying a single-family home where you must wait for the first property to be fully paid before buying a second one.

- Services for managing properties that are financially sustainable.

It is advisable to engage a property manager to handle all the administrative tasks if you lack the necessary administrative abilities or patience to maintain a rental property. Thanks to the multifamily home's good monthly cash flow, you may accomplish that. Whether you purchase a single-family home or a multi-family building, you must make maintenance investments in your buy-and-hold property to attract desirable renters.

## When to Sell a Buy and Hold Property

You should hold your investment properties for at least ten years before selling them unless your investment purpose has changed and you have decided to keep the property permanently. Selling buy-and-hold properties requires considering several criteria.

Let's talk about a few of these elements.

1. Loan term.

When the loan term is about to expire, sell your property.

2. Property market.

See the costs of similar properties in the same neighborhood. If it's a seller's market with high property prices, listing your house for sale is a smart choice.

3. Rent revenue has "frozen".

You might be in a circumstance where increasing the rental fees is difficult, if not impossible. When you get to this point, it is better to sell than to hold onto the property.

4. Increasing property taxes.

You can decide to sell your investment property if the local property taxes are rising to avoid paying high tax rates.

5. A better investment opportunity.

If you are certain that you can use the proceeds to fund a more lucrative endeavor, consider selling your property.

**Making the Buy and Hold Strategy Work**

Despite the simplicity of the buy-and-hold real estate investment strategy, not all investors succeed. So, let us share with you some tips on maximizing your earning potential.

*Choose your property's location wisely.*

To increase the appreciating value of your property, look for neighborhoods where significant economic and infrastructure development initiatives are either underway or will soon be completed.

*Think about purchasing a distressed property.*

To help you reduce the cost of your purchase, foreclosed homes are often sold for less than market value. Search for alternative ways to pay for your property. Be aware that there are other ways to buy a home than just cash. Investigate your options for self-directed IRAs and retirement accounts so you won't have to stress too much about your home payment each month.

*Perform real estate market analysis and investment property analysis.*

These studies ought to help you identify the area and the asset that will yield the greatest profits and enable you to make wise purchase decisions.

*Rent out your property.*

Even if the value of your house rises, you will continue to make money from the monthly rental.

## CHAPTER 10
# FINDING & EVALUATING PROPERTIES: THE DIAMOND IN THE ROUGH

Little indicators can have a major impact when it comes to determining the worth of possible investment properties. Let's look at how to locate the best property with value addition. To determine a reasonable purchase price, numerous aspects relating to a property's potential value must be taken into account. Investors examine local market data, take building and remodeling costs into account, and occasionally can envision a better and more lucrative use than what is already in place. Potential ROI can be considerably increased by being aware of specific value-add indications to look for while searching for commercial real estate.

The following are some signs that a property might be more than it initially appears to be.

**Rents below market rates**

Rent increases are an easy way to increase earnings. There may be an opportunity if a potential investment is charging rent to renters below the going cost in the neighborhood. While assessing a property's potential, it is crucial to take bigger market trends into account.

**Population growth and development in the area**

Population growth is a market factor that needs to be closely monitored. Properties in the neighborhood typically increase in value when the trend is firmly upward. The same is true of the nearby development. The value of investment homes may be greatly impacted by this.

**Old listings or off-market transactions**

Certain high-value discounts can be found by looking at certain kinds of postings. Stale listings that have been sitting on the market for a while are frequently available for much less than the asking price. Also, since there is less competition for those particular homes, an off-market deal might be fantastic.

**Know the area**

By looking into the zoning regulations in a particular area, it may be possible to uncover hidden opportunities in some circumstances. There might be ways to use the land that would enable the conversion of a structure or facility that increases earnings. The size of the lot and its surroundings can also open up growth opportunities, which would increase the property's income.

**Think about other options**

When investors look outside the box, they can add value to homes. Consideration of a location's potential for usage as an Airbnb property, for instance, can be highly helpful in many areas. It can be beneficial to approach each property with an open mind and flexibility.

**Learn the tale**

Investor opportunities may also be found by investigating the mortgage and tenant histories of the property. For instance, the value of that investment is increased by knowing that a rent-controlled renter may be leaving the property shortly. It is given that the rent can be drastically raised in this kind of circumstance. Many different things can affect the prospective profit from a particular piece of property. Investors can create reasonable and competitive offers by being aware of what to search for. Missing out on some incredible offers could result from failing to recognize these indications. Maintaining up-to-date knowledge of market trends, property histories, neighborhood regulations, and construction initiatives will help you spot those gems in the rough.

**How To Find Investment Properties**

For those wondering how to find good investment properties or what to look for, it helps to have a general sense of where to start and what to keep in mind upfront. Following, you'll find some useful hints, tips, and suggestions.

*With A Real Estate Agent*

A real estate agent or licensed REALTOR® can be an important partner in your search for investment opportunities. That's because whether you're interested in flipping houses or buying rental properties, few know the areas or markets that you're looking at shopping is better than a local real estate professional. Bearing this in mind, developing a strong working relationship with a good real estate agent can help lead to a steady source of tips and leads, and help you free up your time to focus more on repairs or property management.

Truth be told, there's little reason to do it alone here, even if you're looking to expand potential investment opportunities by buying foreclosures and REO properties. Between their contacts, connections, and sources of insight, agents can serve as trusted counselors to aspiring real estate investors.

*On The Multiple Listing Service*

The multiple listing service (MLS) can also be one of your best friends, as it offers a comprehensive database of properties for sale in your region. Of course, because everyone else (including other real estate investors) has access to it too, the trick is to be able to act quickly when a property of interest becomes available. That means knowing the area and having proof of funds or a mortgage preapproval letter in place to support any offer that you plan to make. Again, it helps to have a real estate agent (or real estate attorney) handy to answer any questions that you might have if you're ready to make an offer as well.

*Through Online Auctions*

In the age of constant connectivity, apps, and smartphones, online real estate auctions can also be a helpful source of leads and buying opportunities as well. While some real estate auctions still take place on courthouse steps in select states, more often than not, they occur online for buyers to take part in nationwide. Note that auctions generally require aspiring buyers to have enough cash on hand to complete the sale. If needed, you can then arrange for delayed financing to take your cash back out of any projects you've invested in to use for financing future purchases.

**How To Find Off-Market Properties**

Be advised, though: Not every property will appear on the MLS, and many properties (those for sale directly by a motivated owner) may largely be sold via word of mouth. House flippers on the hunt for hidden gems that can be flipped with relatively minimal effort or work for a big profit at resale will especially want to keep an eye out for off-market properties.

*Drive Around*

One of the best sources of potential leads here is simply to drive around a desired neighborhood and stay on the lookout for homes that are up for sale, soon to hit the market or in relative disrepair. Nothing is stopping you from trying the direct approach of knocking on the door or noting the address of the property and looking into it to see who owns it, then contacting the owner to make an appointment. (Hint: You can use the address to look up the owner in public records and databases, or by asking your real estate agent for assistance.) Likewise, you always have the option of putting up signs or fliers in the neighborhood letting property owners know that you're on the lookout for aspiring buys.

*Talk To Everyone*

Similarly, don't underestimate the power of the grapevine and word-of-mouth marketing to drive awareness of the fact that you're shopping around. Letting your real estate agent know to put the word out amongst their network of local professionals is a good idea as well. In addition, while it's important to be respectful of others' feelings and situations, you might also keep an ear out for impending home sales due to a job change, aging parents, or an impending divorce – situations that commonly lead to the sale of homes.

*Visit For Sale By Owner Properties*

If you do spot a For Sale By Owner sign in someone's yard, don't be afraid to seize the moment either. Take the opportunity to make an appointment to visit and tour the property, talk to the owner about any necessary repairs or maintenance, and get a sense of why they're selling. A little legwork can go a long way here to help you get the jump on a prospective buy. In addition, don't forget that many investors still find great real estate deals in their local or target market's Craigslist classified listings, which can often prove an invaluable resource for finding diamonds in the rough that are being offered for sale by the owner.

### Check Out Pre-Foreclosures And Foreclosures Online

Pre-Foreclosures and foreclosures can offer especially good deals and buying opportunities for patient and persistent real estate investors who don't mind putting in a little extra work. Several online websites provide information about these properties to investors, who'll want to run regular searches and keep an eye out for purchases to pounce on, especially at the local or county level.

### Pursue Short Sale Opportunities

Another source of leads when it comes to off-market properties can come if you hear about a homeowner that's in financial distress. In this event, you might consider gently and respectfully reaching out and contacting them to see if they're open to the prospect of a short sale, which may result in a financial win-win for both parties (putting much-needed cash in the seller's pocket and a potentially lucrative real estate opportunity in the buyer's hands). For those considering these types of investments, do keep in mind that short sales usually mean that these homes are being sold as it is.

## What To Look For In An Investment Property

Determining what to look for in a potential investment property depends entirely on your financial goals and plans for new real estate investments. House flippers will naturally want to look for desirable homes in desirable areas that are undervalued, and – with a minimum of time, expense, and effort – can quickly be fixed up and resold for a tidy profit. Rental property investors will instead want to shop for affordable purchases in popular neighborhoods and locations that will be in demand in the future and are likely to attract tenants who can provide a stable, recurring source of passive income as the property appreciates over time. In other words, there are several factors that you'll want to consider when buying your first rental property.

*Location*

You may have heard the oft-repeated phrase that "location is everything in real estate" – mostly because it's true. Owning a desirable property in a popular location in an in-demand area that's on the economic upswing is often the fastest and surest way to ensure a positive return on your real estate investment. Noting this, it's important when shopping around (especially if you're an up-and-coming rental property investor) to look for an area with a steady stream of population influx and prospective renters, like a college town or burgeoning city with a rapidly expanding business district.

*Property Taxes*

Every real estate property owner pays property taxes each year to the federal government. These tax amounts can wax and wane over time. If the property that you're considering comes with high property taxes attached, it can harm annual cash flows, real estate investment profits, and your ability to resell the real estate holding.

*Repairs*

What's more, having to pay for repairs (especially parts and labor) versus being able to perform repairs yourself can also take a big chunk out of your profits. Real estate investors who are unable to perform the necessary tasks of rental property ownership will need to factor in paying for the services of contractors or a property manager. On the bright side, if you're DIY-inclined, you'd be amazed at just how much you can pick up these days when it comes to maintenance and repairs just by checking out online tutorials or watching streaming videos.

*Metrics*

Naturally, it's also important that the numbers add up as well. Investors are strongly advised and encouraged to plot budgets, map out financing figures, and otherwise do the math needed to understand the profit potential of any investment before forking out the purchase price for it. Helpful metrics like projected return on investment (ROI), the internal rate of return (IRR), and the gross rent multiplier (GRM) can help you make more rational vs. emotional or ill-informed decisions here.

## CHAPTER 11
# HOW TO USE OTHER PEOPLES MONEY (OPM)

When we hear about self-made millionaires succeeding on their own, as investors, it's critical to comprehend what exactly is meant by the word "self-made." Most of the time, no one person can build wealth on a million or billion-dollar scale by themselves. Independence is always desirable, but over the last ten years, I've built a million-dollar real estate portfolio and have discovered that these endeavors don't always succeed when we try to do it alone, saving for one sizable down payment at a time. We must use other people's money (OPM) and learn to accept giving up a share of the gain. OPM is a method that banks use extensively for capital raising, lending, and reinvestment. We need to go beyond a bank's capacity to lend to us and instead benefit from their extensive experience in how to safely raise funds, as sophisticated investors with a strong track record.

*Starting a real estate fund with private equity*

Simply put, banks first started to get money by going to a group of investors and trying to get them to trust the bank with their money. In exchange, investors could be sure that their cash would be safe and that they would get interest payments. In the same way, investors can become fund managers once they find investors for a blind pool fund, also called a blank check offering. Real estate investment funds are similar to mutual funds, but most of what they hold are commercial and residential properties instead of stocks or bonds. The value of these funds goes up because of appreciation, improvements to the property, and rental income. When people buy shares, they would get the same help with managing their portfolios as they would with any other mutual fund. As their fund manager, you can use their money to raise more money in any way you want, if you meet the terms of your agreement with them. Most of the time, this means making regular interest payments and sending out a quarterly report or holding regular conference calls to explain what's going on with the investments. Hire a lawyer who specializes in asset management and investment funds to set up the fund structure. These are the professionals who can make sure your fund meets all the security rules.

*Seller Financing*

Some investors might not have the track record of success, or the qualifications needed by a group of fund participants to trust them with managing their hard-earned money.

Investors then need to focus on a smaller pool of prospects. When using seller financing, for instance, to purchase real estate that the seller already owns outright, you only need to gain the confidence of one person: the seller. This sort of financing appeals to sellers because it allows them to sell their homes for more money without having to put any of their own money upfront. The agreement's conditions are typically set up in a promissory note, which, in exchange for a transfer of ownership, permits the buyer to make regular payments toward the loan until they can pay it off in full of a more significant lump sum amount. The buyer still benefits from lower overhead expenses than what a bank would charge them for underwriting, appraisals, or the legal clearance of an application, even if the seller decides to raise the sales price. Also, albeit at a higher expense, the buyer is given a chance they might not have otherwise had.

To ensure they are safeguarded from fraud and have the first lien on the asset, sellers should speak with a real estate attorney.

*Joint Endeavors*

The easier it is to raise money, the fewer people investors need to help them. A proven track record in real estate investing with excellent returns or equity ownership as compelling evidence makes it even simpler. Investors can raise money through joint ventures whenever they have adequate experience and proof of their accomplishment. In my experience, this has proven to be the simplest and most efficient strategy for increasing the wealth of each partner.

Partners prefer this form of arrangement because it gives them greater influence over how the investment is managed and allows them to actively participate in investment activities if they so desire. They might also be silent partners and still have ownership interests as shareholders. The barriers to success are the same regardless of the method used to raise OPM. Ensure that all investors are on the same page and that everyone has a clear understanding of one another's goals from the start. Strive to bring in people with varied backgrounds and degrees of competence; however, avoid bringing together leaders with radically different leadership philosophies since this might easily lead to little or no cooperation. Investors may have difficulty locating OPM, particularly if they lack the track record necessary to demonstrate their potential. Yet, if they are successful in increasing OPM, the advantages are endless. Investors can build their portfolio tenfold, which is something they could never do while working a 9 to 5 job. They may also levy the relevant fees once they have demonstrated their capacity to handle OPM and deliver the results required by their partners. When OPM is developed properly, avoids common problems, and utilizes the appropriate legal framework everyone involved benefits.

**Hard Money Lending**

The first step in breaking down real estate financing is to understand what a hard money loan is and how it works. In the end, hard money loans are a real estate investor's best friend because they are the fastest way to get a deal. Still, hard money lending can get complicated quickly, so you should know what you're getting into before you make a decision. When looking into hard money loans for real estate, you need to know the answers to the following questions:

What are the good and bad things about such a plan?

When is it a good idea to use private financing for a real estate deal?

Where can you locate real estate hard money lenders?

In general, the more you know about hard money, the better. This guide should help you understand everything you need to know about one of the best ways to get money for real estate investors.

*What Is Hard Money Lending?*

Many investors looking for alternative financing that doesn't involve their local bank may have heard the term "hard money." They may have even asked themselves a simple follow-up question: what is hard money lending? Hard money lending is a short-term loan obtained from private investors or individuals at terms that may be stricter than a traditional loan. Though the terms of this creative financing option may be stricter, this form of private financing for real estate generally has more lenient criteria.

*Hard Money Lending FAQs*

1. The Big Picture Of Hard Money Lending

Aside from using conventional mortgage financing, an investor may also use hard money lending to fund their real estate ventures. Instead of other conventional institutions like banks or credit unions, this loan is a short-term one that is secured by private investors or individuals. Investors who want to make improvements to or renovations to a property and then sell it frequently use hard money lending. This is a good option for property flippers and real estate developers because you can typically acquire a loan in a matter of days (as opposed to weeks from banks). This is a choice for investors who just need to make fast improvements to a property's value and then obtain a new loan based on the increased value to pay off the hard money lender.

2. Hard Money Lending Vs. Other Lending Types

The primary distinction between hard money lending and other loan kinds is that the former does not use your income or credit history as collateral. Instead, lenders will emphasize the worth of the property following repairs as the determining criterion (ARV). The ARV of a property is its value after renovations.

Other differences include:

- Hard money lenders do not invest in primary residences. Owner-occupied residential properties are subject to many rules and regulations, thereby increasing the risk for lenders.
- Hard money lenders do not sell loans to Freddie Mac or Fannie Mae. More often than not, lenders use their own money or raise it from a pool of investors. The loan amount is based on their property specialization (if there are any) and the risks they are comfortable taking.
- Hard money loans are short-term. You will not have the luxury of 15 to 30 years to repay your loans. Hard money

loans are typically needing to be repaid anywhere between 6 to 18 months.

- Hard money lenders have their lending criteria. A private lender, for example, could be your friend, family, or business associate. As such, they may not have any preset criteria before lending you money, giving you more flexibility in negotiating terms. Hard money lenders, on the other hand, come with a specific set of upfront points, interest rates, and defined durations.

3. What Are Hard Money Loans Used For?

Hard money loans can be applied for many different types of investments and objectives. Hard money loans are frequently employed in the real estate sector to buy both residential and commercial properties. This is partly due to the conditions for approval and the fact that hard money lenders can operate on the tight schedules that concluding deals frequently demand. Hard money loans are frequently utilized to renovate and resell real estate. Because their ultimate objective is to resell the house for a profit after the renovation is complete, these investors could be less concerned about rising interest rates. Hard money loans are the ideal solution because they can be used to buy houses and undertake improvements.

**The Pros And Cons Of Hard Money Loans**

I firmly believe that hard money loans are one of the most beneficial funding options available to investors. There aren't many financial resources that can compete with hard money and provide the same competitive edge, if any. After all, many investors owe a debt of gratitude to hard money loans for helping them get their initial agreements. Having said that, there are some limitations to hard money. Hard money loans are quick to approve and fund, and they can hasten the entire real estate investing process. They are not suitable for non-real estate investors because they have rates that are significantly higher than those of a typical loan. Although it has greater advantages, hard money has drawbacks that every investor should take into account.

**Pros**

Securing financing with a hard money lending loan offers you several benefits, including:

*Speed:* The Dodd-Frank Act is a financial reform legislation enacted in the past decade. It came with new regulations on mortgage lending, which means a lot of time (often months) is needed for an investor to close a loan. On the other hand, hard money lending is fast, as you can secure a loan in days or weeks (depending on negotiations). Time is essential, especially for large development projects, and hard money lending can help speed that process along.

*Flexibility:* Terms can be negotiated with hard money lending loans since you are dealing directly with individual investors. Banks are not as flexible.

*Collateral:* With hard money financing, the property itself is your collateral for the loan. Some lenders even accept other assets, like your retirement account or residential property under your name, as a basis for starting a loan.

*No "Red Tape":* Getting a loan for an investment property with a traditional mortgage is difficult, if not impossible. Traditional borrowers need to worry about credit scores, LTV ratios, debt-to-income, and several other indicators they need to meet criteria for. However, hard money lenders function as asset-based lenders who are more concerned with the property than the borrower's credentials.

*Convenience:* There is something to be said for the convenience of being able to close with cash. Having to supply a lender with bank statements, income documentation, tax returns, and leases can become overbearing and consume your focus and energy. Hard money, on the other hand, cuts out the middleman and a lot of the headaches.

*Volume:* Hard money lenders allow investors to leverage other people's money. That means investors could potentially fund more than one deal at a time. Traditional loans will do no such thing. If you want to fund multiple deals at a time, you should consider a hard money loan.

*Competitive Edge:* Hard money allows investors to beat out the competition, or at least those using a traditional loan. If for nothing else, sellers prefer the two things hard money offers: cash and a timely transaction.

**Cons**

*Cost:* The convenience that comes with hard money lending may be its primary benefit; however, it is also its main drawback. Since hard money lenders are at higher risk than borrowers, many may demand up to 10 percentage points higher than traditional loans. Interest rates range from 10 to 15 percent. Expect other fees to be also at a relatively increased rate, including origination fees and closing costs.

*Short Repayment Schedule*: A shorter repayment period is the price to pay for being able to get a property listed on the market ASAP. This can be anywhere between 6 to 18 months. Ensure you can sell the property and get your profit as soon as possible.

**Hard Money Loan Rates**

Rates on hard money loans are frequently substantially higher than those on fixed-rate mortgages. Hard money loans often range from 8% to 15% higher than the conventional 3.5% fixed-rate mortgage loan. It's also possible that hard money loans won't cover the entire amount of the asset you want to finance. You might need to put more money down on the property or find another funding source to finish the sale if a hard money loan does not cover the entire value.

## When To Use Hard Money For Real Estate

Even while hard money lenders frequently offer loans for nearly any kind of property, some real estate ventures were developed specifically for this sort of financing. Hard money was designed to be used to finance land loans, construction loans, and rehabilitation projects. For instance, investors require access to money for purchasing and remodeling costs when flipping a house. Since "these projects often develop on a short timeframe, investors do not have time to wait through the procedure of a regular loan approval," it is advised that this is the case. This does not imply that hard money should not be used to finance other kinds of ventures. The speed and simplicity offered by a hard money loan might be priceless if you, the property buyer, have credit problems or you need to act swiftly on a deal before it vanishes. In these circumstances, hard money loans may be used to buy residential or commercial properties.

## Finding Hard Money Lenders For Real Estate Investing

Many new investors fret over how they will find hard money lenders to get moving on the financing of their projects. But here are a couple of simple ways to approach this:

- REIA or Meetup Meetings: Often, hard money lenders will speak at local real estate events. If not, ask fellow members to see if they know any trustworthy lenders.
- Real Estate Agent or Traditional Lender: Ask that realtor or mortgage broker in your real estate network if they know a hard money lender you could do business with.
- Google "Hard Money Lender": Just be careful, there are some unscrupulous individuals out there. Be sure to ask for references and talk to fellow investors to get their opinions.

**How Does Hard Money Lending Work?**

Given that these are private individuals, every hard money lender is different. As stated above, these lenders come with their requirements, including the process they need to close the transaction.

To give you a general idea, this is the usual course hard money lending takes:

1. Find a hard lender near you. Do not let the rejection of a bank loan drive you to desperation. Research and make sure the lender can be trusted. Do they have a legitimate website? Are they in good standing with their investors? Do they have pending lawsuits over bad loans?
2. Arrange a meeting with the lender. This is also the time when you can inquire whether they specialize in a kind of investment property or if they have worked with projects

previously that mirror yours. Assess the time frame specified for the loan and see if this is something you can work with.

3. Prepare a contract. Make sure that you are offering a good deal with a sound financial plan.
4. Inform the lender of your contract price. Most lenders are willing to fund 60 to 70 percent of the property's ARV. The remaining 30 to 40 percent is up to you. You will increase your chances of getting approved if you already have this at hand.
5. Get the property appraised. The lender will either send a list of their trusted appraisers or have their own.
6. Prepare additional documents needed. Some lenders may require that you present other documentation, like W-2s, bank statements, pay stubs, etc.
7. Wait for the lender's approval. If it is a deal that the lender finds satisfactory, then they will inform you of the amount and terms for payment.
8. Consult with a lawyer. Make sure that you are legally protected, especially after getting the lender's counteroffer.
9. Close the loan. Typically, this will be done at a title company or a lawyer's office. The lender will then put the money into escrow at the title company. The title company would make sure all paperwork is completed and that checks are issued to all parties involved. Additional costs may include any closing fees and property insurance.

More often than not, lenders grant money to properties that will not be in the market for long, and that have good selling potential. Make sure your team budgets ample time to complete renovations. There's no sense in coming up with unrealistic projections. This can set you back financially and possibly burn a future relationship with your hard money lender.

**Alternatives To Hard Money Loans**

Hard money loans are not the only form of financing with approval requirements that differ from a traditional home loan. In fact, numerous alternatives may help you buy your next property:

- **Home Equity Loans:** If you are trying to finance your second property (or an investment property), consider tapping into your existing equity with a home equity loan. The approval requirements are largely based on the value of the property and the amount of equity you have built up. These loans are also associated with lower interest rates when compared to hard money loans.
- **FHA Loans:** Federal Housing Administration (FHA) loans are an option for borrowers who do not meet the traditional criteria. FHA loans have lower approval requirements and do not consider past financial challenges (namely bankruptcy) during the application process. Read our guide to FHA loans to learn more.
- **VA Loans:** Loans by the Department of Veterans Affairs require no down payment and have much lower approval

standards. These loans are only provided to qualified veterans, active-duty service members, and their spouses. The interest rates and application requirements are often much more favorable if you do qualify.

www.ingramcontent.com/pod-product-compliance
Lightning Source LLC
Chambersburg PA
CBHW050650160426
43194CB00010B/1889